COLLEGEVILLE BIBLE COMMENTARY

11

THE BOOK

OF

REVELATION

(well thought out event)

Pheme Perkins

THE LITURGICAL PRESS

Collegeville, Minnesota

ABBREVIATIONS

Gen—Genesis
Exod—Exodus
Lev—Leviticus
Num—Numbers
Deut—Deuteronomy
Josh—Joshua
Judg—Judges
Ruth—Ruth
1 Sam—1 Samuel
2 Sam—2 Samuel
1 Kgs—1 Kings
2 Kgs—2 Kings
1 Chr—1 Chronicles
2 Chr—2 Chronicles
Ezra—Ezra
Neh—Nehemiah
Tob—Tobit
Jdt—Judith
Esth—Esther
1 Macc—1 Maccabees
2 Macc—2 Maccabees
Job—Job
Ps(s)—Psalms(s)
Prov—Proverbs

Eccl—Ecclesiastes
Song—Song of Songs
Wis—Wisdom
Sir—Sirach
Isa—Isaiah
Jer—Jeremiah
Lam—Lamentations
Bar—Baruch
Ezek—Ezekiel
Dan—Daniel
Hos—Hosea
Joel—Joel
Amos—Amos
Obad—Obadiah
Jonah—Jonah
Mic—Micah
Nah—Nahum
Hab—Habakkuk
Zeph—Zephaniah
Hag—Haggai
Zech—Zechariah
Mal—Malachi
Matt—Matthew
Mark—Mark
Luke—Luke

John—John
Acts—Acts
Rom—Romans
1 Cor—1 Corinthians
2 Cor—2 Corinthians
Gal—Galatians
Eph—Ephesians
Phil—Philippians
Col—Colossians
1 Thess—1 Thessalonians
2 Thess—2 Thessalonians
1 Tim—1 Timothy
2 Tim—2 Timothy
Titus—Titus
Phlm—Philemon
Heb—Hebrews
Jas—James
1 Pet—1 Peter
2 Pet—2 Peter
1 John—1 John
2 John—2 John
3 John—3 John
Jude—Jude
Rev—Revelation

Nihil obstat: Robert C. Harren, J.C.L., Censor deputatus.

Imprimatur: ✚ George H. Speltz, D.D., Bishop of St. Cloud. July 22, 1982.

Library of Congress Cataloging in Publication Data

Perkins, Pheme.
   The Book of Revelation.

   (Collegeville Bible commentary ; 11)
      1. Bible. N.T. Revelation. English. New American
Bible. 1983. II. Title. III. Series.
BS2825.2.P47   1983   228'.077   83-955
ISBN 0-8146-1311-X

CONTENTS

The Book of Revelation

Introduction

A book for troubled times

The past ten years have seen an explosion of interest in the Book of Revelation at all levels, from that of the biblical scholar down to the casual Bible reader. From one end of the globe to the other, people are asking questions about Revelation. Why the attraction of this complex, often bizarre writing, which seems as far as one could get from our modern world of science and technology? Of course, most of the questions are based on a misunderstanding of Revelation, which assumes that it is a symbolic code predicting the exact persons and events that are leading to the end of the world. This type of understanding has existed in heretical Christian circles since the second century A.D. A group of Montanists even went off into the Phrygian wilderness to see the heavenly Jerusalem descend out of heaven. Like such prophets ever since, they were disappointed in their expectations. The church did not end Sacred Scripture with this book in order to provide glorified predictions of future events.

Anyone who expects predictions of that sort misses the spiritual message of Revelation. It is this spiritual truth that should compel present interest in the book. Despite scientific progress, despite communications media which give us greater and greater access to information and events, despite national and international efforts to relieve human suffering, the world seems more out of joint than ever. Senseless brutality, war, oppression, starvation—wherever we look civilized societies seem to be coming apart at the seams.

Perhaps the best index of our distress is in our movies. The popular movies *Star Wars* and *The Empire Strikes Back* picture a future in which most of the universe has been subjected to evil forces. The "high-tech" background of these movies also mirrors our society. The power of good, "the force," seems reduced to its last card in young, inexperienced, and spiritually undisciplined Luke Skywalker. These movies are not like the old Westerns to which they are often compared. There we always know that the "good guys" will win. They are bigger, better looking, smarter, have better horses, etc. The *Star Wars* movies, on the other hand, no longer provide the good with such an overwhelming advantage. *The Empire Strikes Back* ends with the hint that Luke's own father may have deserted the force to head the empire. Thus, these movies give a striking portrayal of the uncertainty of technological progress and of its futility in the face of evil and spiritual confusion. At the same time, they evoke hope for a time of spiritual renewal.

The Book of Revelation is like such a movie of its time. We find cosmic distances between earth and heaven; the good represented by a small, persecuted group of humans on earth; heavenly aid and inspiration to sustain them; strange, symbolic animals, and cosmic warfare between the forces of good and evil. So, we might ask ourselves what this Christian prophet from the end of the first century has to say to the end of the twentieth. What letters would he be writing to our churches? What would he say about the spiritual disorientation of Christians today? The growing interest in the Book of Revelation shows that people have an instinctual feeling for its message. They are looking for a vision of the struggle between good and evil which does not leave inspiration to modern film-makers or, for that matter, to simplistic prophets of doom.

Revelation as an apocalypse

A person who has never seen the *Star Wars* movies will not understand the comparison in the previous section as well as one who has. Most twentieth-century readers are in a similar position with regard to Revelation. It is full of images that have a long history, stretching from ancient Near Eastern myth through the Old Testament prophets to Jewish apocalypses like the Book of Daniel. These images were also being used and reused in Jewish writings from New Testament times. Some images in Revelation might also evoke Greek mythology, which would be familiar to its readers from the consistent use of such themes in the decorative arts.

Apocalypse is the Greek word for "revelation." From Daniel at the end of the Old Testament to Revelation at the end of the New, and even beyond the time of Revelation, we have a wide variety of such visionary writings from Jewish and Christian circles. They were a form of expression that the audience was familiar with, just as people today are familiar with the *Star Wars* type of film, even if they have not seen the above examples. Read Dan 7–12. Much of the imagery in Revelation derives from Daniel and from the imagery of Old Testament prophets. These chapters of Daniel contain a series of visions of the course of world history. The cycles of visions overlap and provide alternate pictures of the same events. Revelation uses cycles of visions in the same way. Daniel and Revelation are both addressed to a community suffering persecution. When Daniel was written, the Syrian ruler of Palestine had been trying to force people to renounce Judaism. Many who refused were put to death. Reflection on the significance of their martyrdom led to a theology of martyrdom. The blood of these martyrs was seen as expiation for the sins of those Jews who had not remained faithful to their religion.

That theology of martyrdom played an important part in early Christian understanding of the death of Jesus. His blood was seen as an expiation for the sins of the whole world. Revelation presents us with this picture of Jesus as the faithful martyr. He can use the Danielic picture of the faithful martyrs to encourage Christians who face persecution. Just as Antiochus failed to wipe out Judaism, so the new imperial beast, Rome, will fail to destroy the Christian faithful. Notice the image of "one like a Son of Man" ascending to God's throne in Dan 7. Originally, the "Son of Man" who receives dominion over the world referred to the martyrs of Israel. Once again, Revelation is able to apply that image to Christ. Jesus is revealed as the heavenly Son of Man in the opening verses of the book.

The Jewish apocalypses 4 Ezra and 2 Baruch, which were written about the same time as Revelation, address the suffering and spiritual disorientation felt by the Jews after the Romans had destroyed Jerusalem and burnt down the temple. Like Revelation, 2 Baruch includes letters to those who are to receive the revelation. All three apocalypses are concerned with the question of why God does not step in and send the messianic age by destroying evil—especially the Satanic embodiment of evil in the Roman Empire. All three answer with symbolic visions of world history unrolling according to a plan that God has measured out. They promise the faithful that they are much closer to the end of history than to its beginning. They reassure the suffering with the certainty of divine judgment on those who do evil and happiness for those who have endured. Those who have suffered and died out of faithfulness to God are not forgotten. They are enjoying happiness and peace. Though the images and themes of Revelation seem strange to us, these parallel examples show that they were well known at the time the book was written.

All of these apocalypses come from people oppressed by imperial powers. That situation is another reason that they use highly symbolic language, which only people familiar with the tradition of interpreting such images could understand. Criticism of political rulers could be dangerous business. Some ancient philosophers criticized tyrannical political power, but they would often wait until a particular emperor had been assassinated and was out of popular favor before making critical remarks. The Jewish writers use an additional device both to protect themselves and to lend authority to their visions. They present their writings as the secret, recently discovered revelation of a famous person from an earlier time of persecution. Daniel was a wise man at the court of the Babylonian king three centuries earlier. Baruch was a scribe at the time of the Babylonian Exile and an associate of the prophet

Jeremiah. Ezra was a scribe who brought some people back to Palestine from the Exile when the Persians came to power almost a century later. These sages of Israel are claimed to have left symbolic revelations of the future sufferings that had now come upon Israel.

The reader of Revelation will immediately notice a difference. The author does use the tradition of symbolic language and has the evils of Babylon stand for the evils of the Roman Empire, but he does not hide behind a pseudonym. He tells us who he is and where he is: a Christian prophet named John, on the island of Patmos. On the artistic plane, there is an immediacy and sweep to his revelation that is different from his Jewish contemporaries. They engage the revealing angel in extensive dialogues about evil and divine justice. Their visions are said to take place over a lengthy period, often punctuated by periods of fasting and isolation. John's vision does not include such theological dialogue. It appears to happen all at once, so that the reader is swept through scene after scene. Like an epic movie, these scenes are linked together with a dramatic sound track—the chaos and disorder of battle, the thunder of horses, the sound of trumpets, and the beautiful pauses in heaven when the heavenly hosts sing praises to God and to Christ. The onrush does not stop until we find ourselves in the peace of the new Jerusalem.

In this study of Revelation, we will break up the book and trace the background of its symbolic visions. Such a process, however, ruins its dramatic sweep. Try reading the whole through without stopping. It is best to read it through aloud, since most people only came to know Revelation as they heard it read—probably during a liturgical assembly. The details of this study should contribute to that vision of Revelation as a whole.

The author and his situation

People often assume that Revelation was written by the same person who wrote the Fourth Gospel. However, the author does not identify himself as the evangelist. In fact, he even refers to the apostles as a separate group from the past (18:20; 21:14). Even in ancient times people recognized that the two books could not have been written by the same person, since they do not have the same style. But the use of Revelation by heretical groups had led many Christians to be suspicious of it. By treating the John of Revelation as though he were John the evangelist, it was possible to win recognition for Revelation among Christians who might otherwise have rejected it. Today we do not require such a fiction about the author. We recognize that the church has included this writing in Scripture because it does contain an authentic and important vision of Christian faith.

Revelation opens with seven very stylized letters to churches in cities in Asia Minor. However, the author clearly expects that the whole book will be read. That means that all seven letters are intended to instruct all Christians, not just those in the particular churches. Doubtless, Christians living in Asia Minor at the end of the first century were able to understand the symbolic allusions to people and events better than we can today. However, some general problems emerge clearly enough. Some Christians are becoming lax. They seem to have lost interest in testifying to their faith. Others are being led astray by false Christian teachers and prophets, both men and women. It is harder to tell what the references to the "synagogue of Satan" and to "those who claim to be Jews but are not" mean. Some scholars think that the Jewish population of the cities mentioned was responsible for the persecution of Christians. Others suggest that Christians were trying to avoid suspicion and persecution by claiming to be Jewish.

The visions show us faithful Christians who are liable to persecution, and sometimes martyrdom, for failure to worship the emperor. There is no evidence for a formal decree enforcing such veneration throughout the empire. The persecution referred to in Revelation must have been a local phenomenon. Perhaps it was even instigated by local officials or other citizens who wanted to demonstrate their own loyalty to Roman imperial rule. Tradition associates Revelation with the period of the emperor Domitian (assassinated A.D. 96). He emphasized the monarchic side of imperial office and ruthlessly executed those in his own circles whom he suspected of disloyalty. Though he sometimes tried to gain favor in the provinces by removing a particularly unpopular local official and though his rule was a time of prosperity in Asia Minor, he was not universally loved. His assassination was greeted with outbursts of violence against his statues. Clearly, Christians were not the only Roman subjects who were discontented.

People often find it hard to understand "emperor worship." They think that it meant putting the emperor in the place that we reserve for God. Revelation agrees, but most people would have been puzzled by that attitude. Remember, the ancients had many gods. They also believed that some humans were exalted to dwell with the gods after death. Roman art depicts the soul of the emperor being carried up into such heavenly company from the time of Julius Caesar on. Veneration of living emperors began with his successor, Augustus. Often it simply meant using the same language about the emperor and the benefits he bestowed on humanity as was used about the gods in prayers and hymns. Private citizens or individual towns might honor the emperor by establishing holidays and offering sacrifices and holding festal games in his name. They might send an emissary to the emperor's court to inform him of those honors. They hoped, of course, that the emperor would respond by showering his divine favor on their city—perhaps granting relief from some form of taxation. Towns would also vie with their neighbors to see who could come up with the most lavish honors. These practices, then, involved a large measure of civic pride and even local political maneuvering. All this activity was in the hope of gaining some advantage from this distant figure whose statues and images were everywhere, who was felt to control the whole world, and yet whom most people would never see.

Such civic occasions were not the only ones on which a person who refused to venerate the emperor could be exposed to ridicule or suspicion. Elements of emperor worship formed part of everyday life. Slaves and people who had suffered losses in court suits might flee to a statue of the emperor in hopes of obtaining mercy from this distant person who represented "all-seeing" justice. Of course, such hopes were rarely fulfilled, but the mere fact that people had heard stories of people being so helped kept the hope alive. Most formal business and legal transactions were sealed with oaths sworn to the gods and the emperor. People might be asked to swear such an oath when receiving a loan or paying taxes. Local trade guilds might have banquets at which toasts were spoken in honor of the emperor. Perhaps the meal would begin with a libation being poured out in his honor. Even in private homes such libations might be offered at the beginning of the meal.

Jews avoided such situations by avoiding business and social contact with non-Jews. They were well known among non-Jews for their refusal to participate in the various manifestations of civic pride and solidarity. Consequently, they had the reputation of being "haters of humanity." Christians were in a different position. Most belonged to that larger non-Jewish community. Further, they could not carry out the task of witnessing to their faith if they withdrew from contact with the larger world. However, we can see as early as 1 Corinthians that Christians had problems in their social contact with non-Christians. 1 Cor 8 and 10 discuss the various sorts of banquets that a Christian might attend. St. Paul told Christians that they did not have to isolate themselves. They did not even have to avoid meat that had been used in sacrifice to a pagan god and then sold in the market, but they had to avoid compromising their faith in two ways. They could not accept an invitation to a banquet held in a temple honoring a pagan god (1 Cor 10:14-22). While they could accept invitations to the homes of pagan friends and eat whatever was served, they had to refuse to eat meat if someone made a point of telling them that it had been used in a sacrifice to an idol (10:27-32).

St. Paul also tried to deal with the question of Christian loyalty to the political order in Rom 13:1-7. Even though Christians know that all authority is based in God and that Jesus' return will soon bring human authorities to an end, they should still obey those in power, since their role is to see that good is promoted and evil punished. 1 Pet 2:12-17 echoes the same sentiments. Christians are even instructed to "honor the emperor." Since this benign view of political power was widely held in early Christianity, we can presume that it may have contributed to the confusion felt by Christians in Asia Minor. Should they avoid persecution, giving offense, by going along with local customs and demands? What was the difference between not asking questions about the meat and, perhaps, pouring a little libation in honor of the gods? If authorities are to be obeyed, then shouldn't one just swear the oaths required? Considering the social context of emperor worship, how easy it might be for Christians to come to such a conclusion. Perhaps some of the false teachers mentioned in the letters taught Christians that they could make such accommodations. John wants to make it clear that there is a big difference: Using language about the emperor as though he were a god or participating in rituals that honored him as such was equivalent to denying that one is a Christian. That is equivalent to joining forces with Satanic power.

The theology of Revelation

Revelation addressses serious questions about how Christians are to live in a larger, often hostile society. We may not know people today who are compelled to such veneration of political power, but we do not have to look far in the morning paper to read of the harassment or even murder of those who oppose governmental oppression in the name of Christian love and concern for the poor. The most perplexing cases are those in which governments of so-called Christian countries seem to promote policies of oppression that run directly counter to the ethical teaching of Christianity. Revelation speaks about such experiences. It warns us against the temptation to be silent or look the other way in the presence of evil and injustice.

There are also the smaller situations of daily life in which Christians prefer to remain silent and apathetic. Some would require us to act as a group, a church, or group of churches to oppose wrongs in the local community. Others, like the situation of the Christian at a friend's banquet, are more individual. Perhaps we allow people to slander or make fun of what we believe in rather than speak up. We would rather avoid controversy than question opinions, attitudes, and practices that we think are wrong. Of course, sometimes people remain silent because they do not know how to speak in defense of what they believe. People often want to defend their beliefs but lack the words with which to do so. We need to do everything we can to help one another become more articulate believers. After all, as Revelation so often insists, no Christian is immune from the obligation to bear witness.

Finally, the grand sweep of Revelation should lead us to resist the kind of pessimism that looks at the vastness of evil in the world and decides that any effort to change things would be a waste of time. Such judgments are false because Christians are not to measure what is true or right by statistics. Such judgments are arrogant because God is the only one who can determine "what's worth it." Such judgments are demonic because they only contribute to the hold that evil and pessimism have over human lives. Revelation is not a book aimed at scaring Christians into being good. It is a book to encourage them in the face of the most awful shape that evil can assume: when it takes on all the trappings of divine, imperial power; when it also has the force of local opinion behind it; when even some religious leaders are lined up against the few who would resist. Yet, it is the faithful few who share the victory that Christ's death has won over evil.

Structure of Revelation

Revelation has a complex structure. Many scholars think that the author put together vision accounts that were originally separate. While this subject of source analysis is beyond the scope of this commentary, please note that the author announces the next cycle of visions before he is finished with the cycle he is recounting. Such passages are similar to the flashes forward and backward in movies. The broad skeleton of the book seems to be built on the series of seven used to organize the vision cycles. In addition, the visions are presented as the contents of two scrolls: one, opened by the Lamb, dominates chapters 5-10; the other, eaten by the prophet, covers chapters 11-22. The second half of the book also has a dualistic axis embodied in the struggle between God and Satan, which is presented as the contrast between two cities—Babylon (= Rome) and Jerusalem.

OUTLINE OF THE BOOK OF REVELATION

1:1-8	a. Prologue
	Preface (vv. 1-3)
	Prescript and Sayings (vv. 4-8)
1:9-3:22	b. Seven Letters
4:1-8:5	c. Seven Seals
8:2-11:19	d. Seven Trumpets
12:1-15:4	e. Unnumbered Visions
15:5-16:21	f. Seven Bowls
	Babylon Interlude (17:1-19:10)
19:11-21:8	g. Unnumbered Visions
	Jerusalem Interlude (21:9-22:5)
22:6-20	h. Epilogue
	Sayings (vv. 6-20)
	Benediction (v. 21)

The Book of Revelation

Text and Commentary

I: PROLOGUE

1 ¹The revelation of Jesus Christ, which God gave to him, to show his servants what must happen soon. He made it known by sending his angel to his servant, John, ²who gives witness to the word of God and to the testimony of Jesus Christ by reporting what he saw. ³Blessed is the one who reads aloud and blessed are those who listen to this prophetic message and heed what is written in it, for the appointed time is near.

[handwritten margin notes: "Beatitude", "first of 7 beatitudes"]

PROLOGUE

Rev 1:1-18

The prologue has two parts. The first is a titular introduction to the Book of Revelation as a whole (vv. 1-3). The second is an introduction to the first section, the letters to the seven churches (vv. 4-8).

1:1-3 Heed this revelation. The opening words of the book are: "The revelation of Jesus Christ." The word "revelation" has a special meaning here, just as it does elsewhere in the New Testament. It does not refer to any sort of divine inspiration. Rather, it means knowledge of how the world will stand under God's judgment when history comes to an end. Such knowledge does not require detailed predictions about the events or timing of the end of the world, the sort of false interpretation often given of Revelation; what it requires is an understanding of the conditions for salvation, whenever that final judgment comes. We have already suggested in the Introduction that Revelation seeks to correct Christians who are confused about what is required for salvation.

The opening sentence is awkward, since everyone responsible for this revelation is included. The message in Revelation is both a messsage from Jesus to his churches and from God about the coming judgment. The seven letters are tied to a vision of Jesus as the heavenly Son of Man. The visions which follow the letters introduce angelic mediators, who interpret what John sees.

Such angels are a common feature of Jewish apocalypses. As we have already seen, this apocalypse is unusual in being attributed to a living prophet rather than to a famous figure of the past.

Several expressions in this section are used to conclude the book. The promise to show "what must happen soon" (v. 1) reappears at 22:6. In 22:16, Jesus is the one who sends the angel. Similar promises to reveal "what will happen in the last days" appear in Dan 2:28f., 45. There "what is to happen" refers to the destruction of human empires and the establishment of the eternal rule of God. The same structure informs the visions that are to come in Revelation.

Some scholars think that "servants" in verse 1 only refers to a school of Christian prophets who were seeking such visions; however, we agree with those who feel that it refers to all Christians. The next verse pronounces a blessing on all who read, hear, and heed the message. It suggests that Revelation is to be read aloud in the liturgical assembly and is addressed to all. A similar beatitude appears in the conclusion (22:7). The solemn announcement of beatitude in a liturgical assembly carries a note of warning. Those who do not heed the revelation will not find themselves included in salvation. These beatitudes may reflect Luke 11:28, "blest are they who hear the word of God and keep it." Revelation contains the only beatitudes outside the Gospels. In keeping with the number symbolism of the book, there are seven (1:3; 14:13; 16:15; 19:9; 20:6; 22:7, 14). The others refer to the blessings of salvation.

Verse 2 introduces important words in the vocabulary of Revelation, "testimony/witness." The same Greek word underlies both English words. The parallel phrases "word of God" and "testimony of Jesus Christ" suggest that Revelation uses "witness" in a wider sense than that of a martyr who dies for the faith. In verse 9 (RSV) we learn that John was exiled to Patmos "on account of the word of God and the testimony of Jesus" (the New American Bible has interpreted this sentence by adding words that are not in the Greek). Here in verse 2, John places the whole revelation in the category of "word of God and testimony of Jesus." Since he can use the same expression in both contexts, we should presume that the content of this revelation is not a complete surprise. He already holds to the principles that are expressed in these visions. He has already opposed the "beast" in some way. Perhaps he was also worried by the laxity that he saw growing up among Christians. The revelation will bring together and clarify those experiences and concerns. The prophet can say for sure that Christians must not be taken in either by false teachers or the desire to avoid hardship and embarrassment. Instead, they must heed this vision of God as the sovereign ruler of the world.

II: LETTERS TO THE CHURCHES OF ASIA

Greeting. ⁴John, to the seven churches in Asia: grace to you and peace from him who is and who was and who is to come, and from the seven spirits before his throne, ⁵and from Jesus Christ, the faithful witness, the firstborn of the dead and ruler of the kings of the earth. To him who loves us and has freed us from our sins by his blood, ⁶who has made us into a kingdom, priests for his God and Father, to him be glory and power forever [and ever]. Amen.

⁷Behold, he is coming amid the clouds,
   and every eye will see him,
   even those who pierced him.
All the peoples of the earth will lament him.
   Yes. Amen.

1:4-8 A message to the churches. This section begins with the standard opening for a letter. Once again, multiple testimony is behind the message in the coming letters. John is the mouthpiece for God and Jesus. "Grace and peace" was a common early Christian greeting for the opening of a letter. The last verse will come back to this letter introduction with the concluding benediction: "The grace of the Lord Jesus be with all" (22:21). The greeting ends with verse 5a. It is followed by a doxology (vv. 5b-6) and two prophetic oracles.

Balancing lists of titles set off the names of the senders of the letter, God and Jesus. Instead of the standard expression for the divine "is, was, and always will be," God is described as the One "who is and who was and who is to come." The standard formula might be misunderstood. It might suggest that God will not do anything about manifesting his sovereignty over evil. The seven spirits before the throne use Jewish liturgical images. They can have a number of interpretations: seven archangels; the seven eyes of God (so Zech 4:10); seven lights (as in the Jewish apocalypse *2 Enoch* 6, 11). The three parts to the name of Jesus parallel the name of God. "Faithful witness" may refer to all of Jesus' testimony and not simply his death, since Revelation often uses "witness" in a more general sense. "First-born of the dead" refers to Jesus' resurrection. It appears in a hymnic passage celebrating Jesus' cosmic rule in Col 1:18. Finally, "ruler of the kings of the earth" begins to introduce the political overtones of the message. Jesus already rules those who are using their power to harass his followers. The doxology which follows upon verse 5a calls Christians to give glory to Jesus for the salvation that they have received. Doxologies and hymns of praise are an important part of the prophetic insight of Revelation. They teach Christians that they already owe God thanks for his victory and salvation. They do not have to wait until the final destruction of evil for victory.

Two prophetic sayings conclude this section. The first is a combination of Dan 7:13 and Zech 12:10. Early Christians used this saying as a judgment

⁸"I am the Alpha and the Omega," says the Lord God, "the one who is and who was and who is to come, the almighty."

The First Vision. ⁹I, John, your brother, who share with you the distress, the kingdom, and the endurance we have in Jesus, found myself on the island called Patmos because I proclaimed God's word and gave testimony to Jesus. ¹⁰I was caught up in the spirit of the Lord's day and heard behind me a voice as loud as a trumpet, ¹¹which said, "Write on a scroll what you see and send it to the seven churches: to Ephesus, Smyrna, Perga-

oracle against those who reject Jesus (Matt 24:30; John 19:37). Oracles of judgment such as this one have a dual perspective, since they also point to the salvation promised the faithful. Revelation itself is to be read from this perspective. Judgment against evil and its forces represents the salvation of those who are faithful.

The final saying reminds the hearer that this revelation comes from the one who is truly God. Revelation uses "Alpha and the Omega," the first and last letters of the Greek alphabet, for both God and Christ (1:17; 2:8; 21:6; 22:13). "The almighty"*(pantokratōr)* is a divine title (4:8; 11:17; 15:3; 16:7, 14; 19:6, 15; 21:22). It sets God off as king against the power claimed by the empire in the later visions. The liturgical imagery of this section makes it clear from the beginning that this revelation comes with all the authority of God.

LETTERS TO THE CHURCHES

Rev 1:9–3:22

1:9-20 Prophetic call vision. The first vision of Jesus in Revelation commissions the prophet to write to the churches in Asia Minor. Though addressed to specific communities, these messages introduce a revelation addressed to the whole Christian community. The problems in those churches were probably typical of those faced by Christians elsewhere. John's prophetic call is somewhat different from the Old Testament call stories. The Christian prophet is primarily a witness to the message from the risen Jesus. Jesus, not the prophet, is pictured as the one standing over against a wayward people with the words of judgment or consoling the faithful with those of promise.

The prophet makes it clear that he is a member of the community to which this revelation is addressed. "Distress," "the kingdom," and "endurance" present the conditions for Christian salvation. "Endurance" is a special term in the New Testament. It means more than just putting up with hardship. It is the virtue which enables people to remain faithful right through to the end, even though the final days of the world would be characterized by terrible distress and affliction for the righteous. Usually, people think of kingly

mum, Thyatira, Sardis, Philadelphia, and Laodicea." ¹²Then I turned to see whose voice it was that spoke to me, and when I turned, I saw seven gold lampstands, ¹³and in the midst of the lampstands one like a son of man, wearing an ankle-length robe, with a gold sash around his chest. ¹⁴The hair of his head was as white as white wool or as snow, and his eyes were like a fiery flame. ¹⁵His feet were like polished brass refined in a furnace, and his voice was like the sound of rushing water. ¹⁶In his right hand he held seven stars. A sharp two-edged sword came out of his mouth, and his face shone like the sun at its brightest.

¹⁷When I caught sight of him, I fell down at his feet as though dead. He

rule as something that they will share with Jesus only in the future. However, John means more than that. He has already shown that Jesus is ruler of the kings of the earth. Therefore, he can speak of the Christian who endures the sufferings of the last days as already sharing in that rule.

Patmos was a small, poor island with no city on it. John makes it clear that his witness has led to his banishment there. He does not explain the situation further, since the Christians in Asia Minor were probably familiar with the circumstances. Early Christians substituted celebration of the "Lord's Day" for the Jewish sabbath, since it was the day on which Christ rose (see *Barnabas* 15,9; Ignatius, *Magnesians* 9). It was the day on which they met to celebrate the Eucharist (*Didache* 14). Thus, the author sets his visions at the most solemn liturgical time in the Christian week. The voice of God appears as a trumpet in the Old Testament (Ezek 3:12; Exod 19:16). A trumpet call was to signal the end of the world (1 Thess 4:16).

The number seven, which is the primary numerological symbol in Revelation, has many different associations. Some ancient authors would see the seven as the seven planets. The Roman emperor could be portrayed as holding seven stars (= the planets) as symbols of his universal dominion. Consequently, the image of Jesus holding seven stars provides a symbolic challenge to that claim of authority. He is the ruler of the cosmos. In the immediate context of the book, seven refers to the churches to which the letters are addressed (v. 20).

The description of Jesus is not intended as the representation of a visual image. Rather, the seer has brought together a number of images from the Old Testament to express the divine nature and authority of Jesus. The basic image combines the Son of Man who takes the throne in Dan 7:13-14 with the image of God, the Ancient of Days, who gives him that throne (Dan 7:9-10). Other elements in the description come from a vision Daniel has of a revealing angel in 10:5-6. Read those passages. A person familiar with Daniel would immediately recognize that Jesus is presented as an angelic, heavenly being who is both the source of revelation and the one who has

17

touched me with his right hand and said, "Do not be afraid. I am the first and the last, [18]the one who lives. Once I was dead, but now I am alive forever and ever. I hold the keys to death and the netherworld. [19]Write down, therefore, what you have seen, and what is happening, and what will happen afterwards. [20]This is the secret meaning of the seven stars you saw in my right hand, and of

dominion over the world. The sword in the mouth of the figure probably refers to the sword of the word of God (cf. Isa 49:2).

The initial reaction of fear at the appearance of the angelic or divine revealer is common in such visions (Isa 6:5; Ezek 1:28; Dan 8:18; 10:9-11). It is followed by reassurance (Dan 10:12). The description of Jesus had given him some divine attributes. Now he receives the titles of God: "first and last," "the one who lives." He merits these titles because of his death and resurrection.

One theme continuing throughout Revelation is the paradox of death and life. Jesus died and now lives. Those who are not faithful may live now, but they will die later when they are condemned at the judgment. If Christians can remain convinced that Jesus' death/resurrection has reversed the poles of life and death, that there is life far more important than anxious concern for our mortal bodies, then they will not be subject to fear and intimidation. Revelation tries to deal with that fear throughout its visions with vivid, almost grotesque portrayals of the reality of earthly life in contrast to the peace and glory of heaven. We make many decisions that are unconsciously motivated by our fear of dying—either actual death or symbolic death in the loss of something that we love or think we cannot live without. Thus, even if we are not faced with the threat of martyrdom, we still need to examine our own conviction about life/death. Is it really changed, reversed even, by our belief that Christ died and now lives? Or is it the same anxious concern with present self and security that motivates those who have no faith?

Some interpreters try to argue that the "angels of the churches" refers to the bishops of those communities. However, the letters never suggest that they are directed toward specific church leaders. Therefore, we would agree with those who assume that Revelation is thinking of the angelic guardians of those churches along the lines of Jewish speculation of the time which held that angels had been assigned to the different nations of the earth. This perspective also fits in with another feature of Revelation: The truth of external earthly events is found in the action in heaven which initiates them.

The letter pattern

The letter section provides prophetic evaluation, critique and encouragement to the churches mentioned. Each letter follows a pattern:

the seven gold lampstands: the seven stars are the angels of the seven churches, and the seven lampstands are the seven churches.

2 To Ephesus. ¹"To the angel of the church in Ephesus, write this:

" 'The one who holds the seven stars in his right hand and walks in the midst of the seven gold lampstands says this: ²"I know of your works, your labor, and your endurance, and that you cannot tolerate the wicked; you have tested those

1. Command to write.
2. Prophetic messenger formula with a description of Jesus as the sender.
3. "I know" section.
   It includes some of the following elements: (a) "I know that" + description of the situation; (b) "But I have it against you" (censure); (c) command to repent; (d) "Look" + prophetic saying; (e) promise: the Lord is coming soon; (f) exhortation to hold fast.
4. Call to hear.
5. Promise of reward to those who are victorious.

These letters do not give us much information about the problems in the churches of Asia Minor. They speak in a cryptic way about situations that were familiar to the original audience. Their message is a prophetic warning that Christians must take care lest they lose the salvation that Christ has won for them.

Ignatius, the bishop of Antioch, wrote letters to churches in the same area about two decades later (ca. A.D. 110). They show that some of the same problems mentioned in these letters continued to plague the churches in that area. Ignatius mentions heretical teachers. He says that they were denying that Christ was really human. They were also challenging the authority of the local church leaders. Other Christians are continuing to follow Jewish customs. They refuse to believe any teaching which is not contained in the Old Testament. The opposition in Ignatius' time seems to be more doctrinally oriented and better organized than that in the letters in Revelation. However, that strong opposition may have been the continuation of trends that are beginning as Revelation is written. If so, John's stern warnings against the false teachers is certainly justified. They would continue to plague the church.

2:1-7 To Ephesus. The city of Ephesus had undergone a great revival during the Roman period. That renewal would have given the populace reason to be enthusiastic about the empire. Consequently, we are hardly surprised to find this civic pride manifested in devotion to the emperor. At the same time, this city was also an important Christian center, since it had been part of the Pauline mission in Asia Minor.

who call themselves apostles but are not, and discovered that they are impostors. ³Moreover, you have endurance and have suffered for my name, and you have not grown weary. ⁴Yet I hold this against you: you have lost the love you had at first. ⁵Realize how far you have fallen. Repent, and do the works you did at first. Otherwise, I will come to you and remove your lampstand from its place, unless you repent. ⁶But you have this in your favor: you hate the works of the Nicolaitans, which I also hate.

⁷" ' "Whoever has ears ought to hear what the Spirit says to the churches. To the victor I will give the right to eat from the tree of life that is in the garden of God." '

To Smyrna. ⁸"To the angel of the church in Smyrna, write this:

" 'The first and the last, who once died but came to life, says this: ⁹"I know your tribulation and poverty, but you are rich. I know the slander of those who claim to be Jews and are not, but rather are members of the assembly of Satan. ¹⁰Do not

The description of Jesus reminds the reader of 1:13, 16. The letter opens by praising this community for its endurance and its resistance to false teachers who claim to be apostles. Revelation usually limits the term "apostle" to the Twelve (so 18:20; 21:14). Presumably, people claiming to be apostles were using the term as it had been used during the time of Paul in reference to traveling missionaries (cf. Rom 16:7). Perhaps these traveling missionaries had been preaching the doctrines of the Nicolaitan sect mentioned in verse 6.

Though not in danger from false teachers, the Ephesian community has to be recalled to its former enthusiasm. The image of a fall from its former heights may have been based on the image of the fallen star in Isa 14:12a. The lampstand image recalls the single lampstand with seven lamps in Zech 4:2, which is in the divine presence. Revelation threatens Ephesus with removal of its lampstand.

The call to hear which forms a set part of the conclusion to the letters is a common prophetic warning. (It also appears in Rev 13:9; 21:7; 22:2.) The promise, eating from the tree of life, appears in first-century Jewish apocalypses as well. It shows that salvation reverses the curse of Adam. Revelation has already shown its audience that lost immortality is regained through Jesus.

2:8-11 To Smyrna. Smyrna was a fairly new city north of Ephesus. It had a sizable Jewish population. When its bishop, Polycarp, was martyred in A.D. 155, conflicts between Christians and Jews were blamed. This letter leads off with the theme of life through death to encourage the suffering community. However, we cannot be sure whether Jews were the ones responsible for that suffering. It is possible that some Christians were trying to escape persecution by keeping to Jewish customs. (Compare the reference to those who will not admit to believing in Jesus because they prefer human glory

be afraid of anything that you are going to suffer. Indeed, the devil will throw some of you into prison, that you may be tested, and you will face an ordeal for ten days. Remain faithful until death, and I will give you the crown of life. [11]" ' "Whoever has ears ought to hear what the Spirit says to the churches. The victor shall not be harmed by the second death." '

To Pergamum. [12]"To the angel of the church in Pergamum, write this:

" 'The one with the sharp two-edged sword says this: [13]"I know that you live where Satan's throne is, and yet you hold fast to my name and have not denied your faith to me, not even in the days of Antipas, my faithful witness, who was martyred among you, where Satan lives. [14]Yet I have a few things against you. You have some people there who hold to the teaching of Balaam, who instructed Balak to put a stumbling block before the Israelites: to eat food sacrificed to idols and to play the harlot. [15]Likewise, you also have some people who hold to the teaching of [the] Nicolaitans. [16]Therefore, repent. Otherwise, I will come to you quickly and wage war against them with the sword of my mouth.

in John 12:42-43.) Revelation must encourage this church to endure because more suffering awaits it. The "crown of life" image may be a combination of the crown of precious stones placed on the head of the righteous (Ps 21:4) and Yahweh as crown of hope (Isa 28:5). The audience might also have imagined it as similar to the crown given to victorious athletes.

Verse 11 explains the death that Christians really should fear: condemnation in the judgment or "the second death." They can avoid that death only by remaining faithful in their present suffering.

2:12-17 To Pergamum. Pergamum was an important city in Asia Minor. Its famous temple to Caesar was placed on a high, terraced hill. The city was known for its devotion to the cult of Augustus Caesar and the goddess Roma. This reputation for devotion to the emperor cult has earned the city the epithet "throne of Satan" in the eyes of the prophet. Perhaps refusal to participate in some form of that civic cult led to the death of the famous martyr Antipas.

The church is chided for following the teachings of the Nicolaitans. They are compared to the Israelites when they were misled by the false prophet Balaam (Num 25:1; 31:6). Some interpreters suggest that this sect might have taught that Christians could engage in ceremonial acknowledgments honoring the emperor. The condemnation of their eating "food sacrificed to idols" might indicate participation in ceremonial banquets, for instance. Ostensible paticipation would win such Christians freedom from persecution. They may have felt that such rites were not worship, since they did not believe that the emperor was divine. Revelation reverses their evaluation. Any form of participation in imperial cult is worship of Satan.

The promises of salvation pick up the two themes for which some are being condemned. Christians saw the "manna" as a prefiguration of the Eu-

[17]' "Whoever has ears ought to hear what the Spirit says to the churches. To the victor I shall give some of the hidden manna; I shall also give a white amulet upon which is inscribed a new name, which no one knows except the one who receives it." '

To Thyatira. [18]"To the angel of the church in Thyatira, write this:

" 'The Son of God, whose eyes are like a fiery flame and whose feet are like polished brass, says, this: [19]"I know your works, your love, faith, service, and endurance, and that your last works are greater than the first. [20]Yet I hold this against you, that you tolerate the woman Jezebel, who calls herself a prophetess, who teaches and misleads my servants to play the harlot and to eat food sacrificed to idols. [21]I have given her time to repent, but she refuses to repent of her harlotry. [22]So I will cast her on a sickbed and plunge those who commit adultery with her into intense suffering unless they repent of her works. [23]I will also put her children to death. Thus shall all the churches come to know that I am the searcher of hearts and minds and that I

charist, which in turn prefigures the final messianic banquet with Christ in heaven. The victors are also promised a new name. In Phil 2:6-11, Jesus receives the new name "Lord" when he is exalted in heaven. The new names received by the faithful are part of their share in the victory of Christ when they will eat the heavenly banquet. For the time being, both the manna and the new names remain hidden in heaven, but that should not cause Christians to abandon their glorious salvation.

2:18-29 To Thyatira. This city was less important than the previous three. Its citizens had lost their bid to have the emperor's temple built there instead of in Pergamum.

The church in this city appears to have been severely divided. The author encourages those members of the community who are remaining faithful. He castigates others who are following the teachings of a woman prophet. He calls her "Jezebel," after King Ahab's pagan wife, who caused her husband to worship the pagan god Baal (1 Kgs 16:31). He threatens her and her followers (= children; perhaps even disciples as prophets, just as in the Old Testament a disciple of a prophet might be a "son of a prophet," see Amos 7:14). Jewish traditions frequently link sexual immorality with idolatry. Consequently, the combination does not provide us with any specific information about her group. We are told that they claim to know the "deep things" (RSV) of Satan, according to the author of Revelation. They must have claimed to know the deep things of God. Such an expression in a Jewish apocalypse of the period would most naturally express the claim to know the secrets surrounding the end of the world and the judgment. Perhaps their visions also legitimated participation in pagan cult. John's revelation will provide the true Christian knowledge of such deep things. The followers of this false prophecy are reminded that they must repent; nothing can be hidden from God who knows all (Jer 17:10). The violence of the punishments against

will give each of you what your works deserve. [24]But I say to the rest of you in Thyatira, who do not uphold this teaching and know nothing of the so-called deep secrets of Satan: on you I will place no further burden, [25]except that you must hold fast to what you have until I come.

[26]' "To the victor, who keeps to my ways until the end,
I will give authority over the nations.
[27]He wil rule them with an iron rod.
Like clay vessels they will be smashed,

[28]just as I received authority from my Father. And to him I will give the morning star.

[29]' "Whoever has ears ought to hear what the Spirit says to the churches." '

3 To Sardis. [1]"To the angel of the church in Sardis, write this:

" 'The one who has the seven spirits of God and the seven stars says this: "I know your works, that you have the reputation of being alive, but you are dead. [2]Be watchful and strengthen what is left, which is going to die, for I have not found your works complete in the sight of my God. [3]Remember then how you accepted and heard; keep it, and repent. If you are not watchful, I will come like a thief, and you will never know at what hour I will come upon you. [4]However, you have a few people in Sardis who have not soiled their garments; they will walk with me dressed in white, because they are worthy.

[5]' "The victor will thus be dressed in white, and I will never erase his name from the book of life but will acknowledge his name in the presence of my Father and of his angels.

[6]' "Whoever has ears ought to hear what the Spirit says to the churches." '

To Philadelphia. [7]"To the angel of the church in Philadelphia, write this:

the woman and her followers corresponds to the seriousness of their sin, perverting the true gift of prophecy. However, those in the community who do continue to resist Jezebel and her children will share not only the victory celebration but also the actual rule of Christ over the nations.

3:1-6 To Sardis. Rebuilt after it had been leveled by an earthquake in 17 B.C.E., this city was a famous port for the reshipment of woolens. The promise that the victors will go clothed in white (v. 5) may be an allusion to the city's wool trade. We cannot be sure what had given this city the reputation of "being alive" although it is really dead. Perhaps the Christians there were known for enthusiasm or spiritual gifts. The letter warns that they could lose everything if they do not pay attention to the commandments. Their deeds are not those of Christians. Since the author does not mention any specific faults or false teachers, the problem with this church may simply be a waning of their initial devotion. Each of the promises to the faithful contains a warning to those who are not faithful. They might find their names erased from the book of life. The author reminds them of two judgment sayings attributed to Jesus. He will deny those who deny him (Matt 10:32). They must watch out for the thief in the night (Matt 24:42-44; also as a warning of impending judgment in 1 Thess 5:2).

" 'The holy one, the true,
    who holds the key of David,
    who opens and no one shall close,
    who closes and no one shall open,
says this:
[8]" ' "I know your words (behold, I have left an open door before you, which no one can close). You have limited strength, and yet you have kept my word and have not denied my name. [9]Behold, I will make those of the assembly of Satan who claim to be Jews and are not, but are lying, behold I will make them come and fall prostrate at your feet, and they will realize that I love you. [10]Because you have kept my message of endurance, I will keep you safe in the time of trial that is going to come to the whole world to test the inhabitants of the earth. [11]I am coming quickly. Hold fast to what you have, so that no one may take your crown.

[12]" ' "The victor I will make into a pillar in the temple of my God, and he will never leave it again. On him I will inscribe the name of my God and the name of the city of my God, the new Jerusalem, which comes down out of heaven from my God, as well as my new name.

[13]" ' "Whoever has ears ought to hear what the Spirit says to the churches." '

3:7-13 To Philadelphia. This small city lay in the earthquake zone to the southeast of Sardis. The church is not censured, but it is warned to hold out against those who claim to be Jews but are not. We cannot tell if this controversy was between Christians and Jews over who were the real people of God, the true Israel, or an internal conflict between those to whom Revelation is addressed and a group of Jewish Christians. Just as the author spoke of Pergamum as "Satan's throne" because of the emperor cult, so the Jewish problem here leads him to speak of their gathering as "Satan's assembly" or synagogue. Apocalypses of this type frequently designate opponents of God with Satan epithets. The use of Satan in both letters does not mean that the problem here is the same as in Smyrna.

Revelation alludes to several messianic prophecies to prove that Jesus is the true successor to David. Isa 22:22-25 seems to be the closest to this prophecy, since it refers to the key and the open door: "I will place the key of the House of David on his shoulder; when he opens, no one shall shut, when he shuts, no one shall open." Since the door is still open before this community, they still have the possibility of salvation if they continue to hold out. The letter even promises that the truth of their belief will be demonstrated when some of those who claim to be Jews are converted. Like the calls for repentance in other letters, this promise reminds us that the letters in Revelation are not proclaiming a fate that is already sealed. It is not too late for those being censured to repent. Those who are faithful must be encouraged to continue.

The concluding promises look forward to the coming of the new Jerusalem, which will conclude the visionary section of Revelation. Isa 22:23 makes the messianic steward a sure peg on which the whole weight of his

To Laodicea. ¹⁴"To the angel of the church in Laodicea, write this:

" 'The Amen, the faithful and true witness, the source of God's creation, says this: ¹⁵"I know your works; I know that you are neither cold nor hot. I wish you were either cold or hot. ¹⁶So, because you are lukewarm, neither hot nor cold, I will spit you out of my mouth. ¹⁷For you say, 'I am rich and affluent and have no need of anything,' and yet do not realize that you are wretched, pitiable, poor, blind, and naked. ¹⁸I advise you to buy from me gold refined by fire so that you may be rich, and white garments to put on so that your shameful nakedness may not be exposed, and buy ointment to smear on your eyes so that you may see. ¹⁹Those whom I love, I reprove and chastise. Be earnest, therefore, and repent.

²⁰" ' "Behold, I stand at the door and knock. If anyone hears my voice and opens the door, [then] I will enter his house and dine with him, and he with me. ²¹I will give the victor the right to sit with me on my throne, as I myself first won the victory and sit with my Father on his throne.

²²" ' "Whoever has ears ought to hear what the Spirit says to the churches." ' "

father's house can hang. Again, the victors are promised a new name. Here we learn that the name is that of the victorious Jesus.

3:14-22 To Laodicea. Also in the earthquake belt, Laodicea lies east of Ephesus. We have completed our circle of cities. There had been a church in this area from the time of Paul (Col 4:13). This final letter is most often quoted for its imagery of "lukewarmness." Laodicea's water supply came from hot springs and arrived in the city lukewarm. The prosperity of the city and its trade form the basis for other images used by the prophet. It was known for its clothing industry, as a banking center, and for its medical school, which specialized in eye diseases. The problems of the church in this city are tied to the material prosperity in which Christians here live. They are neither poor nor suffering, but their prosperity is endangering their spiritual well-being.

The prophetic warnings draw on several images from the Old Testament. Only they can obtain gold who will pass the test of divine fire from Jesus. The Lord promises to separate the bad from the good among his people by refining them like precious metal in Zech 13:9. The promise of garments of salvation to cover the shameful nakedness of the people refers not only to the clothing industry of the city but also to the reversal of a prophetic curse: God will strip his enemies and expose their shameful nakedness. Isa 47:1-3 connects this curse with an image of the people as "bride." We will see that that imagery returns at the conclusion of the vision section. The new Jerusalem will be the true bride of the lamb. Ezek 16:8-14 describes Israel as a young bride decked out for her wedding to the Lord. The bridal imagery appears in this passage because the first promise is a share in the divine wedding feast. The culmination of all promises of salvation in Revelation is a share in the victory which the lamb has won. Here the victors are promised a seat on the throne of Jesus and his Father at the festal celebration. Though the letters have been addressed to specific cities, both their warnings and their promises of salvation can apply to all Christians.

SEVEN SEALS

Rev 4:1–8:5

A new vision introduces the next section of the book. Some interpreters think that the letters and the visionary cycles were originally independent and were only combined when the book of visions we know as Revelation was put together. Even if they were originally independent, the imagery of the two sections fits together. The letters presuppose the visions of salvation that are coming in order to make their promises and warnings clear. We would not know that the concern with idolatry and with the throne of Satan refers to the emperor cult without the account of the beast in chapter 13, for example.

The various cycles of visions which make up the rest of Revelation overlap. The trumpets are introduced before the seals are concluded, and almost two chapters stand between the sixth and seventh trumpet. Apocalypses commonly included repetitious cycles of visions, which went over the same ground from a different perspective. The interlocking of the various cycles in Revelation suggests that its visions do the same.

Apocalypses also wish to show their audience that they are nearer to the end of the world than to its beginning. Symbolically, they make this point by having visions that encompass the past history of Israel. These past events may be from the salvation history of the Old Testament and/or from the recent experiences of the people under the Babylonian and Persian Empires such as we find in the visions of Daniel. In that way the audience can see the divine truth behind those past events and can be reassured that the future is no less subject to divine rule, however chaotic and confusing it may seem.

Revelation follows the same process. While reading through the visions carefully, notice that most of them have already been fulfilled from the standpoint of the author and his audience. One should never pay any attention to an interpretation of Revelation that applies to contemporary people and events the images which the author claims apply to the past. Revelation wants us to understand that the same divine judgment and guidance that were manifest in those past events are at work today, not that those past events have to be repeated in some way. When apocalypses come to describe the future

Overlooking the town of Hora on the island of Patmos is the Monastery of St. John the Theologian (above). From the monastery one enjoys a pleasant view of the harbor town of Skala (below). Partially hidden on the slope to the left is the Monastery of the Apocalypse, on the site where the seer of Revelation is supposed to have had his visions (Rev 1:9).

Across the silted-in harbor of ancient Ephesus, behind the grove of trees, are the ruins of the great temple of Artemis, one of the Seven Wonders of the ancient world (see Acts 19). Beyond the white mosque in the center are the extensive ruins of the Basilica of St. John the Evangelist. Prominent on the hill to the left are the ruins of a Byzantine fortress.

Ruins of the great theater at Ephesus, said to have accommodated 25,000 persons. Here the mob gathered against St. Paul, as recorded in Acts 19.

The acropolis at Pergamum (modern Bergama). Pergamum was one of the seven churches addressed by the seer in the Book of Revelation (Rev 2:12-17), where it is called the "city where Satan has his home" (Rev 2:13). It was one of the early sites of emperor worship and a chief center of worship of the healing god Asklepios.

Ruins of the agora at Smyrna (modern Izmir), also one of the seven churches addressed in Revelation. The philosopher Apollonius of Tyana (d. 98) referred to Smyrna's "crown of porticoes," a circle of splendid public buildings that decorated the summit of Mount Pagos like a diadem.

III: GOD AND THE LAMB IN HEAVEN

4 **Vision of Heavenly Worship.** ¹After this I had a vision of an open door to heaven, and I heard the trumpetlike voice that had spoken to me before, saying, "Come up here and I will show you what must happen afterwards." ²At once I was caught up in spirit. A throne was there in heaven, and on the throne sat ³one whose appearance sparkled like jasper and carnelian. Around the throne was a halo as brilliant as an emerald. ⁴Surrounding the throne I saw twenty-four others thrones on which twenty-four elders sat, dressed in white garments and with gold crowns on their heads. ⁵From the throne came flashes of lightning, rum-

events of judgment/salvation, they often move away from any connection to historical events and speak in the language of mythological symbols and metaphors. Revelation does the same. This shift in language reminds us that the seer is having a vision of the divine or symbolic truth that is to be worked out in the course of history. He is not trying to predict a sequence of historical events as they might be recorded in a history book or a newspaper.

It would also be a mistake to think that the imagery of wrath and punishment is the real foundation of Revelation. Both the letters and the visions make it clear that they seek to encourage Christians to remain faithful in a difficult and confusing time. Remember, John even has to contend with other Christian prophets who claim that they know the "deep things" of God. Revelation does not seek to teach Christians to glory in the expectation that others will suffer a terrible fate while they rest in the bliss of heaven. John sees that the victory that has been won in Christ is the beginning of a divine process of redemption that is to take in all of creation. Throughout the book hymns of rejoicing and celebration invite Christians to celebrate their salvation.

4:1-6a The divine throne. The Old Testament contains several visions of the heavenly throne and its surroundings. They introduce the mission of a prophet whose experience in the heavenly court gives him the authority to speak God's word to the people (1 Kgs 22:19; Isa 6:1-13; Ezek 1:4-26; Dan 7:9-10). Read the Ezekiel passage. It shows how familiar the scene in Revelation would be to a person who knew the earlier images. Not only is the vision of God's throne room a customary beginning for a prophetic revelation, but it also reminds the audience of this book of one of its major themes: God, not Caesar, is the ruler of the cosmos. The final letter promised that Jesus and his faithful ones would even share the divine throne at that final victory banquet. The next vision will show us the victorious enthronement of the lamb.

Visions of heaven often begin with the invitation to enter or to look through the open door into heaven (Ezek 1:1; Matt 3:16; Acts 7:56). Though the visions follow the letters, the author does not imply that everything in

blings, and peals of thunder. Seven flaming torches burned in front of the throne, which are the seven spirits of God. ⁶In front of the throne was something that resembled a sea of glass like crystal.

In the center and around the throne, there were four living creatures covered with eyes in front and in back. ⁷The first creature resembled a lion, the second was like a calf, the third had a face like that of a human being, and the fourth looked like an eagle in flight. ⁸The four living creatures, each of them with six wings, were covered with eyes inside and out.

the letters has to happen before the events described in the visions will begin. The promise to show "what must take place in time to come" is the customary introduction to an apocalypse. As we have noted, such apocalypses may still contain visions that begin in the past, describe persons and events known at present to the audience, and then look to the future.

The seer has been commissioned in the visions which opened the book. After this first cycle of visions is over, he will be commissioned again. Now he provides a vision of the divine throne room. The scene combines images of the temple of Solomon in the Old Testament (see 2 Chr 3–5), throne of cherubim, brazen sea, incense, singing, and altar of sacrifice, with the scroll image of the synagogue, its elders and hymns, and the imagery of the heavenly court assembled in judgment (as in Dan 7:9-14). The crowns and white robes suggest that the twenty-four elders represent human rather than angelic figures. Some commentators think that they may represent the prophets of Israel.

The author has combined images of heavenly liturgy with those of the heavenly court assembled in judgment. When the lamb opens the scroll in the next scene, we see that judgment has begun to unroll. The piling up of images makes it clear where power and authority lie. Between the throne and the elders the image of the divine is manifest in a great storm. The seven torches are the seven spirits of God which ovesee the whole cosmos (Rev 5:6; see Zech 4:2). The bronze sea reflects that which stood before the temple of Solomon. It symbolizes the creative power of God, which is victorious over the sea of chaos. The cosmological mythology of the sea as the home of a great monster of chaos, which must be defeated by the divine storm god before the world can be created, becomes even more explicit later in Revelation. The empire is embodied in the beast which comes from the sea. God as creator imposes order by defeating the sea monster.

4:6b-8 The four heavenly creatures. In Ezek 1:4-20 the prophet first sees a great storm wind. Within it he finds the throne chariot of God being drawn by four creatures. Ezekiel supposes that each creature has four faces: man, lion, ox and eagle. Revelation has assigned one face to each of the four throne bearers. The images may have been taken from Babylonian signs of the

Salvation is the biggest battle against evil.

Day and night they do not stop exclaiming:

"Holy, holy, holy is the Lord God almighty,
who was, and who is, and who is to come."

[9]Whenever the living creatures give glory and honor and thanks to the one who sits on the throne, who lives forever and ever, [10]the twenty-four elders fall down before the one who sits on the throne and worship him, who lives forever and ever.

They throw down their crowns before the throne, exclaiming:

[11]Worthy to you, Lord our God,
to receive glory and honor and power,
for you created all things;
because of your will they came to be and were created."

5 **The Scroll and the Lamb.** [1]I saw a scroll in the right hand of the one who sat on the throne. It had writing on both sides and was sealed with seven seals.

Ezek 9; seal 1 → page 39 underlined

zodiac. The ox, Taurus, is an earth sign; the lion, Leo, a fire sign; the third, with the face of a man, may be Scorpio, since the scorpion was often drawn with a human face, and is a water sign. The eagle provides a sign for the fourth element, air. It also provides another sign of divine sovereignty over the Roman Empire. Thus the four creatures not only serve to identify the divine throne chariot but also proclaim divine rule over the four elements of the cosmos and over the signs of the zodiac. The final verse brings in the vision of the throne room in Isa 6:1-2. The creatures merge with the cherubim and seraphim of that scene. Later Christians gave each of the four evangelists one of the creatures as a symbol.

4:8b-11 The heavenly praises. The transition to the Isaiah vision is continued with the singing of the threefold "holy." God is glorified by all in heaven as the sovereign creator. This praise makes the implications of the symbolism clear: God is the creator and Lord of all that exists. Several writings from Jewish groups in the New Testament period contain descriptions of the divine throne and of the praises of angels in heaven. The liturgical setting suggests that the acclamations offered by worshipers on earth are an image of the real worship of God which takes place in heaven.

5:1-7 The Lamb receives the scroll. We now turn from praising the divine creator to the plan of redemption. In Ezek 2:9-10, the seer is shown a scroll, which was "covered with writing front and back, and written on it was: Lamentation . . . and woe." That scroll was unrolled before the seer so that he could see what was written on it. Revelation has introduced a slightly different image. The scroll is sealed. That image reflects the revelation of Daniel. There the visionary is told to seal up his revelation: "As for you, Daniel, keep secret the message and seal the book until the end time; many shall fall away and evil shall increase" (12:4). John's question about who can unlock the scroll really is addressed to such apocalyptic visions. It rejects

33

²Then I saw a mighty angel who proclaimed in a loud voice, "Who is worthy to open the scroll and break its seals?" ³But no one in heaven or on earth or under the earth was able to open the scroll or to examine it. ⁴I shed many tears because no one was found worthy to open the scroll or to examine it. ⁵One of the elders said to me, "Do not weep. The lion of the tribe of Judah, the root of David, has triumphed, enabling him to open the scroll with its seven seals."

⁶Then I saw standing in the midst of the throne and the four living creatures and the elders, a Lamb that seemed to have been slain. He had seven horns and seven eyes; these are the [seven] spirits of God sent out into the whole world. ⁷He came and received the scroll from the right hand of the one who sat on the throne. ⁸When he took it, the four living creatures and the twenty-four elders fell down before the Lamb. Each of the elders held a harp and gold bowls filled with incense, which are the prayers of the holy ones. ⁹They sang a new hymn:

"Worthy are you to receive the scroll
and to break open its seals,

the possibility that any apocalypse, any revelation except the Christian one, could unlock the secrets of God's plan for the end of the world. Thus, he makes it clear that as the successor to the prophets Ezekiel and Daniel, he is also the last. The hidden book is now to be opened by the Lamb and the unfolding of the final stages in the history of salvation can begin. The angel issues the summons to the whole cosmos to witness the opening of the book, a feat that cannot be performed by any creature in the cosmos.

The messianic prophecy of the Lion of Judah answers the call. The messiah is now present and worthy to open the book. 4 Ezra 11:36-46 has the Lion emerge and speak the sentence of doom against the fourth imperial beast, the Roman eagle. Here the opening of the scroll by the victorious Lion will begin the visions that spell the end of imperial power. Revelation combines other images with that of the Lion of Judah, the sprout of David from Isa 11:1-10, and the more general messianic image of victory. The Christian audience knows that the victory won by Christ was in his death and resurrection. This fact is symbolized in the vision of the messianic lion as the slaughtered lamb. Several images have been combined. Early Christian traditions identified Jesus with the passover lamb and with the defenseless servant of Isa 53:7, 10-12. In another Jewish apocalypse, 1 Enoch, the seer sees the Lamb of David grow into a great horned sheep, which defeats the hostile beasts that attack the people of God (89, 45-46; 90, 9-16). The Lion of Judah/Lamb in this vision also appears with the horns of a victorious ram. He has the flaming eyes of the seven spirits before the throne (1:4; 3:1; 4:5).

5:8-14 Praises for the Lamb. Once again, we hear the heavenly chorus sing praises. "New song" often appears in the call to worship in the psalms. Here it has the added significance of offering praise to the victorious Lord, enthroned in heaven. He has created a new people of God from all those

for you were slain and with your
blood you purchased for God
those from every tribe and tongue,
people and nation,
¹⁰You made them a kingdom and priests
for our God,
and they will reign on earth."

¹¹I looked again and heard the voices of
many angels who surrounded the throne
and the living creatures and the elders.
They were countless in number, ¹²and
they cried out in a loud voice:

"Worthy is the Lamb that was slain
to receive power and riches, wisdom
and strength,
honor and glory and blessing."

¹³Then I heard every creature in heaven
and on earth and under the earth and in
the sea, everything in the universe, cry
out:

"To the one who sits on the throne and
to the Lamb
be blessing and honor, glory and
might,
forever and ever."

¹⁴The four living creatures answered,
"Amen," and the elders fell down and
worshiped.

IV: THE SEVEN SEALS, TRUMPETS, AND PLAGUES, WITH INTERLUDES

6 **The First Six Seals.** ¹Then I watched
while the Lamb broke open the first
of the seven seals, and I heard one of the
four living creatures cry out in a voice like
thunder, "Come forward." ²I looked, and
there was a white horse, and its rider had
a bow. He was given a crown, and he
rode forth victorious to further his victories.

on earth. Thus, the universality of God's cosmic rule is echoed in the universal
redemption won by the atoning death of the lamb.

As we hear the praises, the author widens the angle of vision so that we
see the myriads of heavenly beings and then all creatures at the various levels
of the cosmos praising the Lamb. Their praise is confirmed with the answer-
ing AMEN of the four throne creatures and the worship of the elders. The
vision of the praise offered by all creation forms a high point in the book.
It is the heavenly basis for the confidence that Christians are to have in the
truth of the visions of divine victory that are to follow. The Lamb has already been enthroned victorious in heaven because he has won a new kingdom of priests. The Christian is shown that the whole cosmos praises God
and the Lamb for their saving power.

6:1-8 The four horsemen. Revelation uses images which flow into one
another. We have seen this process at work in the earlier descriptions of the
divine. When the author now turns to describe the inner reality of earthly
events, he blends together the mythic symbols, the prophetic allusions, and
the hints at the historical events to which they correspond. The four horsemen allude to a very concrete set of experiences of people living in a war-
torn area, the disasters wrought by wars and invading armies. The white
horse and the bow were favorite weapons of Rome's hated enemy along the
eastern frontier, the Parthians. Later, the Parthians are summoned by the

³When he broke open the second seal, I heard the second living creature cry out, "Come forward." ⁴Another horse came out, a red one. Its rider was given power to take peace away from the earth, so that people would slaughter one another. And he was given a huge sword.

⁵When he broke open the third seal, I heard the third living creature cry out, "Come forward." I looked and there was a black horse, and its rider held a scale in his hand. ⁶I heard what seemed to be a voice in the midst of the four living creatures. It said, "A ration of wheat costs a day's pay, and three rations of barley cost a day's pay. But do not damage the olive oil or the wine."

⁷When he broke open the fourth seal, I heard the voice of the fourth living creature cry out, "Come forward." ⁸I looked, and there was a pale green horse. Its rider was named Death, and Hades accompanied him. They were given authority over a quarter of the earth, to kill with sword, famine, and plague, and by means of the beasts of the earth.

voice of God to come from beyond the Euphrates and initiate the downfall of Rome (9:13-21). The vision predicts that Parthian attacks would bring the downfall of Rome. That expectation was a reasonable one, since Rome had suffered defeat at the hands of Parthia in A.D. 62. Parthia would not be the nation to sack Rome, but Rome would eventually fall through war with an enemy on her borders.

The images of a company of horsemen also evoke the prophets. Zech 1:8-15; 6:1-8 pictures riders on different colored horses sent to range the earth and to punish those who oppress the people of God. The terrors of war in these first visions all fit the periods of conflict in the region. The eruption of Vesuvius (A.D. 79) was followed by a devastating fire and plague in the city of Rome and by famine in Asia Minor.

The prophets also picture the horrors of war, famine, plague, and wild beasts as chastisement from God. Ezek 5:12-17 has God utter a terrible curse, which is the basis for this section. In Ezekiel the destruction will kill a third of the people by plague and hunger; a third by war; and the remaining third will be scattered in exile. Perhaps because there are so many more plagues to come, Revelation has its version of the Ezekiel curse carry off a quarter of the earth. The third horseman images the disorienting economic effects of war that might lead some to starvation. The fourth horseman represents death by plague. All of the evils brought by the horsemen referred directly to common experiences in the life of the region through its combination of prophetic images.

6:9-11 The fifth seal. This scene forms an interlude between the plagues of war and the destructive earthquakes of the next scene. It also introduces the theme of the martyr. Those who have suffered call out for vengeance. This cry is not a manifestation of personal animus or spite as some people often think. It is also a common feature of the apocalypse genre: the right-

9When he broke open the fifth seal, I saw underneath the altar the souls of those who had been slaughtered because of the witness they bore to the word of God. 10They cried out in a loud voice, "How long will it be, holy and true master, before you sit in judgment and avenge our blood on the inhabitants of the earth?" 11Each of them was given a white robe, and they were told to be patient a little while longer until the number was filled of their fellow servants and brothers who were going to be killed as they had been.

12Then I watched while he broke open the sixth seal, and there was a great earthquake; the sun turned as black as dark sackcloth and the whole moon became

eous make a call for God to give some definitive manifestation of his justice and truth. This manifestation would counter the appearances of a world which seems able to ignore God's justice without any ill effects, a world which can persecute or simply ignore those who speak out for God. The plagues brought by the four horsemen serve to remind the audience that the world is not as peaceful or prosperous as it might be.

The position of those calling out for vengeance reflects that of the Old Testament "just ones" between the temple and the altar in Matt 23:35. The prayer to God to come and avenge the blood of the righteous alludes to Ps 79:5-6, 10. That psalm was a prayer to the Lord not to continue being angry with his people but to avenge them against the enemies that had laid waste the nation. The words are those of a nation laid waste by war and its devastation; it can only call out to God for help. Here the martyrs are asking God to pronounce sentence on the rightness of their cause and to execute judgment. The visions in Revelation that began with the opening of the scroll make it clear that God has pronounced his sentence against the wicked. But he does not promise immediate execution of judgment. More is yet to come. People often object to the tone of this passage, which seems to make God something of a sadist, unwilling to act until enough righteous blood has been shed. The New American Bible translation contributes to that impression by rendering the Greek "they are fulfilled" as "until the number was filled." The passage is not really about a quota. Apocalypses are concerned with the problem of righteous people who seem to suffer and die needlessly in God's cause. They often reassure their audience that such suffering is not endless, not going to go on forever, by imagining that there is a fixed time period or a set sequence of events that must transpire. Neither the righteous nor the wicked can force the events of history out of that pattern. It is part of the mystery of the divine plan. Revelation does not relish suffering. The book is built around the image of the Messiah as the sacrificed Lamb. Those who suffer for the sake of righteousness are assured that God is attending to their cause; their sufferings and struggles are acknowledged in heaven.

like blood. ¹³The stars in the sky fell to the earth like unripe figs shaken loose from the tree in a strong wind. ¹⁴Then the sky was divided like a torn scroll curling up, and every mountain and island was moved from its place. ¹⁵The kings of the earth, the nobles, the military officers, the rich, the powerful, and every slave and free person hid themselves in caves and among mountain crags. ¹⁶They cried out to the mountains and the rocks, "Fall on us and hide us from the face of the one who sits on the throne and from the wrath of the Lamb, ¹⁷because the great day of their wrath has come and who can withstand it?"

7 **The 144,000 Sealed.** ¹After this I saw four angels standing at the four corners of the earth, holding back the four winds of the earth so that no wind could blow on land or sea or against any tree. ²Then I saw another angel come up from the East, holding the seal of the living God. He cried out in a loud voice to the four angels who were given power to damage the land and the sea, ³"Do not damage the land or the sea or the trees until we put the seal on the foreheads of

6:12-17 The sixth seal. This vision of cosmic catastrophe piles up all the metaphors that the author can find for the horrors of the final day of judgment. Compare the vision of the judgment in Mark 13:4-19. Several Old Testament prophecies are behind this passage. It begins with the earthquake as the sign of divine theophany (see 1 Kgs 19:11; Isa 29:6). This sign would be familiar to many of the audience, since several of the cities addressed were in an earthquake zone. There are to be signs in the stars and the moon (Joel 3:4); darkness (Isa 50:3); falling stars (Isa 34:4). The terrible cry of people for the hills to fall and cover them also appears in the prophetic traditions (Hos 10:8 ties it to the earthquake; Isa 2:10, 19; Jer 4:29). The "great day" of verse 17 appears in Isa 2:10, 19 (also Zeph 1:14). The question posed by this terrible vision, "Who can withstand it?" (see Nah 1:6; Mal 3:2) will be answered by the sealing of the righteous in the next chapter. Thus, the author has piled together all the horrors of the judgment as they were known from the biblical tradition. Those horrors form a prelude to the sealing, which assures the righteous that they can withstand, just as they have withstood persecution in the world.

7:1-8 Seal the 144,000 from the tribes of Israel. Normally, the announcement of the terrible day of judgment would be followed by the vision of the divine theophany, God coming forth in judgment. Revelation breaks into that pattern to answer the question of who can withstand by describing the sealing of two groups. Interpreters are divided over the identity of the 144,000. Some think that they represent the righteous of Israel. Other argue that they represent Christians, who could also speak of themselves as the "twelve tribes" (as in Jas 1:1). Such a Jewish Christian tradition may underlie this passage in Revelation.

Several passages in the Old Testament use the imagery of sealing to indicate that a person belongs to the people of God. Exod 28:11, 21 associates

the servants of our God." [4]I heard the number of those who had been marked with the seal, one hundred and forty-four thousand marked from every tribe of the Israelites: [5]twelve thousand were marked from the tribe of Judah, twelve thousand from the tribe of Reuben, twelve thousand from the tribe of Gad, [6]twelve thousand from the tribe of Asher, twelve thousand from the tribe of Naphtali, twelve thousand from the tribe of Manasseh, twelve thousand from the tribe of Simeon, twelve thousand from the tribe of Levi, twelve thousand from the tribe of Issachar, [8]twelve thousand from the tribe of Zebulun, twelve thousand from

the tribe of Joseph, and twelve thousand were marked from the tribe of Benjamin.

Triumph of the Elect. [9]After this I had a vision of a great multitude, which no one could count, from every nation, race, people, and tongue. They stood before the throne and before the Lamb, wearing white robes and holding palm branches in their hands. [10]They cried out in a loud voice:

"Salvation comes from our God, who is seated on the throne,
and from the Lamb."

[11]All the angels stood around the throne and around the elders and the four living

that sign with deliverance from the disaster of the final plague. The Egyptian plagues will appear later in the visions. Isa 44:5 describes a sealing of the Lord's chosen ones as writing the names "I am the Lord's," "Jacob," and "the Lord's" on the hand. We have seen that in the letters Revelation promises the victorious that they will be given a new name which is that of God, of the new Jerusalem, and of Jesus' own "new name" (3:12). Ezek 9:4 instructs one of those who are to scourge the city of idolaters to pass through first and mark the foreheads of all those who lament the abominations being practiced there with an "X" so that they will not be touched in the coming disasters. In addition to all of these Old Testament examples of sealing and salvation, the Christian audience would also remember their own tradition, which spoke of baptism as "sealing."

God is holding back the four angels who are about to let loose the divine storm winds. They will come from the four corners of the earth as signs of divine wrath (see 1 Kgs 19:11; Jer 49:36; Ezek 37:9; Zech 6:5).

7:9-12 The elect praise the Lamb. On the basis of the Ezekiel parallel, we might expect the new vision of doom to follow immediately. Remember we are still waiting for the seventh seal to bring this first vision cycle to a conclusion. However, Revelation is not simply a prediction of disaster. It also shows the heaveny basis of salvation and Christian hope. Consequently, we are shown a new vision. Just as in the previous vision of cosmic praise, the angle of vision widens until we see multitudes from all the earth praising the Lamb. All of the elect are singing praises and waving palms, a sign of victory (1 Macc 13:37, 51; John 12:13). As in the earlier glimpse of the heavenly liturgy, the hymn is antiphonal. The praises of the elect are answered

creatures. They prostrated themselves before the throne, worshiped God, ¹²and exclaimed:

"Amen. Blessing and glory, wisdom and thanksgiving,
honor, power, and might
be to our God forever and ever. Amen."

¹³Then one of the elders spoke up and said to me, "Who are these wearing white robes, and where did they come from?" ¹⁴I said to him, "My lord, you are the one who knows." He said to me, "These are the ones who have survived the time of great distress; they have washed their robes and made them white in the blood of the Lamb.

¹⁵"For this reason they stand before God's throne

experienced salvation

and worship him day and night in his temple.
The one who sits on the throne will shelter them.
¹⁶They will not hunger or thirst anymore,
nor will the sun or any heat strike them.
¹⁷For the Lamb who is in the center of the throne will shepherd them
and lead them to springs of lifegiving water,
and God will wipe away every tear from their eyes."

8 **The Seven Trumpets.** ¹When he broke open the seventh seal, there was silence in heaven for about half an hour. ²And I saw that the seven angels who stood before God were given seven trumpets.

by heavenly beings who say "Amen" and then offer their own song to God and to the Lamb.

7:13-17 Interpretation of the vision. Interpretation of the seer's vision by an angel is common in apocalypses (compare Ezek 37:3). This passage combines allusions to Ezekiel and Daniel. The tribulation through which these people have passed may be that of the judgment (Dan 12:1), which has just been announced. Verses 15-17 are somewhat problematic, since they seem to narrow the focus of the vision from all the elect to just those who have died for their faith. However, the author may be thinking of all as having a share in martyrdom, since they have been redeemed by the blood of the Lamb.

Several images of salvation from the Old Testament describe what awaits the elect. The righteous will not hunger and thirst (Isa 49:10; Ps 121:6). The sheep will have their shepherd (Ezek 34:23; Ps 23). God will wipe away the tears of the elect (Isa 25:8). Now that we have seen the salvation won for all the elect by the death of Jesus, we are ready for the opening of the final seal.

8:1-5 The seventh seal. The account of the seventh seal includes a verse which introduces the next cycle, the trumpets (v. 2). This interlocking is typical of the style of Revelation. We expect a grand, perhaps terrifying, vision of the divine warrior to follow the announced judgment. Trumpets belong to the announcement of the beginning of judgment (as in 1 Thess 4:16). They announce the appearance of the Lord. Thunder and light-

The Gold Censer. ³Another angel came and stood at the altar, holding a gold censer. He was given a great quantity of incense to offer, along with the prayers of all the holy ones, on the gold altar that was before the throne. ⁴The smoke of the incense along with the prayers of the holy ones went up before God from the hand of the angel. ⁵Then the angel took the censer, filled it with burning coals from the altar, and hurled it down to the earth.

There were peals of thunder, rumblings, flashes of lightning, and an earthquake.

The First Four Trumpets. ⁶The seven angels who were holding the seven trumpets prepared to blow them.

⁷When the first one blew his trumpet, there came hail and fire mixed with blood, which was hurled down to the earth. A third of the land was burned up, along with a third of the trees and all green grass.

ning are also signs of divine presence. However, we do not have the terrifying epiphany of the Lord; instead, there is a half-hour silence followed by further prayers. The silence may reflect the "small voice" of the appearance to Elijah (1 Kgs 19:11-12; 2 Chr 2:17; Hab 2:20). Amos 9:1 pictures the Lord standing beside the altar as he announces to the prophet the judgment he is to bring against his people. Here an angel is offering up the prayers of God's people. Since that offering is followed by his hurling the burning coals down on the earth, we assume that the prayers are the same as those of the martyrs in the earlier chapter. God's people have asked for salvation; the symbolic response shows that their prayer is to be answered.

THE SEVEN TRUMPETS

Rev 8:6-11:19

This cycle is structured like the previous one. Four trumpets herald plagues to come upon the earth. The movement toward the culmination in which Satan is cast out of heaven is interrupted. First we see two faithful witnesses and their fate. Then the prophet is again commissioned by an angel and so prepared for the revelations which form the second half of the book. As in the previous series, the first four trumpets are a short, unified group, while the last three are longer and more diverse. This series is modeled on the plagues of Egypt. It teaches a sobering lesson. The plagues and disasters do not lead to repentance. Instead, the humans who survive continue in their idolatrous ways. This cycle is more intense than the previous one; a third rather than a quarter of the earth is to be affected.

8:6-13 The first four trumpets. The humans who survive this succession of plagues do not realize that they are suffering divine punishment. This series, like the earlier one, presents disasters which are not those of the final judgment. The vision combines images from various Old Testament prophecies

41

⁸When the second angel blew his trumpet, something like a large burning mountain was hurled into the sea. A third of the sea turned to blood, ⁹a third of the creatures living in the sea died, and a third of the ships were wrecked.

¹⁰When the third angel blew his trumpet, a large star burning like a torch fell from the sky. It fell on a third of the rivers and on the springs of water. ¹¹The star was called "Wormwood," and a third of all the water turned to wormwood. Many people died from this water, because it was made bitter.

¹²When the fourth angel blew his trumpet, a third of the sun, a third of the moon, and a third of the stars were struck, so that a third of them became dark. The day lost its light for a third of the time, as did the night.

¹³Then I looked again and heard an eagle flying high overhead cry out in a loud voice, "Woe! Woe! Woe to the inhabitants of the earth from the rest of the trumpet blasts that the three angels are about to blow!"

9 **The Fifth Trumpet.** ¹Then the fifth angel blew his trumpet, and I saw a

with the plagues of Egypt. Ps 18:13 ties the appearance of God to save his people with casting fire and coals on the earth. Blood recalls the plague in Exod 9:24. The second trumpet announces the destruction of the fish in the sea (see Exod 7:18). The image of disaster created by a burning mountain falling into the sea has both historical and prophetic overtones. For the audience at the time, it might evoke the eruption of Vesuvius in A.D. 79, with its rivers of molten lava flowing into the sea and destroying everything in their wake. A burning mountain also appears in Jer 51:25. The Lord will send a destroying mountain against the empire of Babylon.

Allusions to the overthrow of Babylon continue in the next trumpet. The falling star recalls the taunting of the king of Babylon in Isa 14:12. In Jeremiah (23:15; 8:14; 9:14), the Lord threatens to give poisoned water, wormwood, to his people because they have abandoned his ways and gone astray into idolatry. The darkness of the final trumpet in this group recalls the darkness over the land of Egypt (Exod 10:21-29). The prophets frequently refer to the darkness of the day of judgment (Amos 8:9; Isa 13:10; 50:3; Joel 2:3, 10; Ezek 32:7-8). However, this darkness does not represent that of the final day; only a third of the heavenly bodies lose their light.

The first cycle of disasters recalled the trials of international wars. This cycle, disasters in nature, might be called forth by divine command. Verse 13 brings it to a culmination with the ominous vision of the eagle flying across midheaven and crying out three "woes" against the inhabitants of earth (compare the "woe" introduction to prophetic oracles of doom as in Amos 5:7-27, a prophetic announcement of three woes). The vision of the eagle in midheaven may also recall the comparison of the coming of the Son of Man in judgment to eagles/vultures gathering above a corpse in Matt 24:28. The woes announce the next three trumpets. Two will be described immediately; the third will be delayed as in the previous cycle.

star had fallen from the sky to the earth. It was given the key for the passage to the abyss. ²It opened the passage to the abyss, and smoke came up out of the passage like smoke from a huge furnace. The sun and the air were darkened by the smoke from the passage. ³Locusts came out of the smoke onto the land, and they were given the same power as scorpions of the earth. ⁴They were told not to harm the grass of the earth or any plant or any tree, but only those people who did not have the seal of God on their foreheads. ⁵They were not allowed to kill them but only to torment them for five months; the torment they inflicted was like that of a scorpion when it stings a person. ⁶During that time these people will seek death but will not find it, and they will long to die but death will escape them.

⁷The appearance of the locusts was like that of horses ready for battle. On their heads they wore what looked like crowns of gold; their faces were like human faces; ⁸and they had hair like women's hair. Their teeth were like lions' teeth, ⁹and they had chests like iron breastplates. The sound of their wings was like the sound of many horse-drawn chariots racing into battle. ¹⁰They had tails like scorpions, with stingers; with their tails they had power to harm people for five months.

9:1-12 The fifth trumpet. With the fifth trumpet we move out of the realm of earthly disasters into that of the mythological. Mythological beasts come forth to attack the inhabitants of the earth. As though we were watching a horror movie, these creatures come out of the earth to torture humanity. Though the fifth trumpet recalls the plague of locusts (Exod 10:13-15), these locusts are not the ordinary sort of grasshopper that sweeps across fields destroying crops. A great star falling from heaven, possibly Satan, has the keys to let these creatures out of the underworld. They do not harm nature, the grass, at all. Instead, they are sent to torment humanity. They are really scorpion-like creatures. Scorpions were known as "fiery dragons" (Deut 8:15; Num 21:6; Isa 14:29). The prophetic pattern for this vision can be found in Joel 1:4, where the locusts and grasshoppers are sent against humanity. However, Revelation has moved out of the realm of that prophecy, which describes a possible natural disaster, into the realm of the mythological and demonic. Their sting torments but does not kill. The intensity of human suffering at this plague leads to a repetition of the cry of the sixth seal: people wish to die and cannot. (Compare Jer 8:3; Job 3:21; the most horrible suffering leads people to seek death, which they cannot find.)

Some of the features in the description of the locusts come from Joel: teeth, flight, warrior's attire and comparison with war horses (1:6, 2:4-5). The human face was part of the traditional iconography of the scorpion. Perhaps the woman's hair was also derived from astral symbolism. The golden crown will appear later in the crown of the beast. The leader of these creatures is probably the same angel/demon whose fall brought their release from Hades. They torment humanity for five months. Another cry of woe and warning brings this vision to its close.

[11]They had as their king the angel of the abyss, whose name in Hebrew is Abaddon and in Greek Apollyon. *destruction* [12]The first woe has passed, but there are two more to come.

The Sixth Trumpet. [13]Then the sixth angel blew his trumpet, and I heard a voice coming from the [four] horns of the gold altar before God, [14]telling the sixth angel who held the trumpet, "Release the four angels who are bound at the banks of the great river Euphrates." [15]So the four angels were released, who were prepared for this hour, day, month, and year to kill a third of the human race. [16]The number of cavalry troops was two hundred million; I heard their number. [17]Now in my vision this is how I saw the horses and their riders. They wore red, blue, and yellow breastplates, and the horses' heads were like heads of lions, and out of their mouths came fire, smoke, and sulfur. [18]By these three plagues of fire, smoke, and sulfur that came out of their mouths a third of the human race was killed. [19]For the power of the horses is in their mouths and in their tails; for their tails are like snakes, with heads that inflict harm.

[20]The rest of the human race, who were not killed by these plagues, did not repent of the works of their hands, to give up the worship of demons and idols made from gold, silver, bronze, stone, and wood, which cannot see or hear or walk. [21]Nor did they repent of their murders, their magic potions, their unchastity, or their robberies.

10 **The Angel with the Small Scroll.** [1]Then I saw another mighty angel come down from heaven wrapped in a

9:13-21 The sixth trumpet. A new contingent of demonic creatures appears. These terrible horsemen do not signal earthly disasters; they attack and kill a third of humanity. The angelic voice from the altar announces the time for the release of these destroying angels. Such an angelic cry is associated with the trumpet announcing the day of judgment in 1 Thess 4:16. The association between the voice and the altar also reminds the readers of the plagues as answer to the prayers of the righteous. But this woe is not the end of the world, either. Only a third of the inhabitants of the earth are killed. These terrible riders are deliberately more lethal than the previous group. They slay with the fiery breath of their mouths and with the venom of their serpent-like tails.

In these two visions Revelation has moved beyond the metaphors of the Old Testament prophets and beyond metaphorical description of the horrors that might accompany natural disasters or human wars. The author has now moved into the realm of the mythological, of the demonic and of the terrifying. That move makes the conclusion of this series even more sobering. Even attack by such mythic beasts does not change humanity. The conclusion remains much the same as it had been throughout the Old Testament: those who are hardened against the word of God do not repent, no matter what happens to them. Suffering does not convert them. Terror does not convert them. Those who live through such times continue in idolatry and sin. More signs must occur before a terrified humanity recognizes that God is at work (11:13).

cloud, with a halo around his head; his face was like the sun and his feet were like pillars of fire. [2]In his hand he held a small scroll that had been opened. He placed his right foot on the sea and his left foot on the land, [3]and then he cried out in a loud voice as a lion roars. When he cried out, the seven thunders raised their voices, too. [4]When the seven thunders had spoken, I was about to write it down; but I heard a voice from heaven say, "Seal up what the seven thunders have spoken, but do not write it down." [5]Then the an-gel I saw standing on the sea and on the land raised his right hand to heaven [6]and swore by the one who lives forever and ever, who created heaven and earth and sea and all that is in them, "There shall be no more delay. [7]At the time when you hear the seventh angel blow his trumpet, the mysterious plan of God shall be ful-filled, as he promised to his servants the prophets."

[8]Then the voice that I had heard from heaven spoke to me again and said, "Go, take the scroll that lies open in the hand

10:1-7 The small scroll. Once again we must wait for the final woe, the seventh trumpet. The seer will be commissioned once again, and those who are to be witnesses to God's actions in the last days will be established. God will not commence those final events without further prophetic testimony. This vision brings us back to the prophet Ezekiel. The cloud and the rain-bow are signs of divine presence (Ezek 1:28). The angel's face shines with the glory of God. All the demonic images that we have just seen are erased in this new vision of the divine. The scroll scene will rework the scene in which the prophet eats a scroll in Ezek 2:8-3:3. Cries of thunder and the lion's roar both appear as signs that the day of judgment is beginning in the prophets (Amos 1:2; 3:8; Joel 4:16). The seven thunders also remind us of the seven spirits of God.

But the end is not yet. The prophet is not allowed to reveal what is said by the thunders. Daniel seals up the mysteries of his revelation (12:4) be-cause they are for the generation that will live in the last days, not for the people at the time in which the book is said to have been written, several hundred years before the events to which it alludes. John, however, was not such a fictional work. It begins as a revelation to a Christian prophet well known to the audience, not as the words of a wise man long dead. The seal-ing up of what John hears suggests that it is not yet the end time. Lest the audience become alarmed by that new sign of delay, the angel swears an oath by God that the time of the end, the time of the seventh trumpet, is not far off. When that time comes, everything that God has announced to the prophets will come to pass.

10:8-11:12 Commissioning the prophet. The section in which John is commissioned again for the visions ahead recalls two actions from Ezekiel: eating a scroll and measuring the temple. Like Ezekiel, John is instructed to eat a scroll which tastes like honey (Ezek 2:8-3:3). The bitterness [NAB:

of the angel who is standing on the sea and on the land." ⁹So I went up to the angel and told him to give me the small scroll. He said to me, "Take and swallow it. It will turn your stomach sour, but in your mouth it will taste as sweet as honey." ¹⁰I took the small scroll from the angel's hand and swallowed it. In my mouth it was like sweet honey, but when I had eaten it, my stomach turned sour. ¹¹Then someone said to me, "You must prophesy again about many peoples, nations, tongues, and kings."

11 **The Two Witnesses.** ¹Then I was given a measuring rod like a staff and I was told, "Come and measure the temple of God and the altar, and count those who are worshiping in it. ²But exclude the outer court of the temple; do not measure it, for it has been handed over to the Gentiles, who will trample the holy city for forty-two months. ³I will commission my two witnesses to prophesy for those twelve hundred and sixty days, wearing sackcloth." ⁴These are the two olive trees and the two lampstands that

"sour"] in the stomach recalls the bitterness of having to announce the day of the Lord (Zeph 1:14). Verse 11 is awkward: "they" [NAB: "someone"] tell the prophet that he must prophesy again. He is set over against nations and kings (as in Jer 1:10). Yet, we have not yet seen the prophet fulfill the first commission. The verse may simply be an awkward transition between the two different allusions to the prophet's vocation as being like that of Ezekiel.

Measuring the temple of God appears in Ezek 40:3. The prophet measures the temple in view of the fact that it is to be restored. Here the prophet's measuring represents preservation of part of the temple in the period leading up to the end time. The three and a half years during which the outer court is under Gentile dominion is roughly the 1290 days during which the temple was profaned in Dan 12:11. Dan 7:25 has three and a half years as the time during which the fourth and final beast will dominate the saints of God. In Dan 12:7, the revealing angel swears an oath by the Most High (compare the oath of the angel at 10:5-6), that the period of domination by this final empire will be three and a half years. Thus, the audience of Revelation would know that the vision is invoking that earlier tradition. Preservation of part of the temple from domination symbolizes preservation of a remnant, the holy ones of God. The saying in verse 2 may reflect an older Jewish oracle about the destruction of the temple, just as we find an oracle about the "times of the Gentiles" in Luke 21:24. As they hear these prophecies, both author and audience know that the Roman imperial armies had completely leveled the temple in Jerusalem almost a quarter century earlier. They were not looking for precise predictions about the time of domination, or they would not have preserved the Danielic three and a half years. They could see this prophecy as one of those historical allusions to the past which show that the events described and the expectations for the future all belong to the times in which they live.

stand before the Lord of the earth. ⁵If any-one wants to harm them, fire comes out of their mouths and devours their ene-mies. In this way, anyone wanting to harm them is sure to be slain. ⁶They have the power to close up the sky so that no rain can fall during the time of their prophesying. They also have power to turn water into blood and to afflict the earth with any plague as often as they wish.

⁷When they have finished their testi-mony, the beast that comes up from the abyss will wage war against them and conquer them and kill them. ⁸Their corpses will lie in the main street of the great city, which has the symbolic names, "Sodom" and "Egypt," where indeed their Lord was crucified. ⁹Those from every people, tribe, tongue, and nation will gaze on their corpses for three and a half days, and they will not allow their corpses to

11:3-14 Sign of the two witnesses. The dominion of the Gentiles is matched by the sign of the two witnesses. Two probably refers to the num-ber of witnesses required by law. It is difficult to determine who the two witnesses are. Ezekiel has to prophesy against two false advisors to the city in 11:1-4. The witnesses to God might be an antitype to such false advisors. Other interpreters suggest that the two represent the two eschatological prophets Moses and Elijah. The signs that they perform recall Moses' send-ing the plagues on Egypt and Elijah's closing the heavens (1 Kgs 17:1). Verse 4 identifies the witnesses with the lampstand and olive trees that the prophet Zechariah saw next to the Lord (Zech 4:3, 11, 14). No human enemy can attack these witnesses, but they meet their death at the hands of a mythical beast. He is the beast from the sea who fights against God's holy ones in Dan 7:3-7, 19, 21. Here we have another example of Revelation's fondness for interlocking cycles of visions. This beast will be back in chapters 13 and 17. He is embodied in Roman imperial power and its deadly conflict with the truth of God's sovereignty.

Further allusions to Ezekiel structure the rest of the section. In the midst of Ezekiel's prophecy against the two false teachers, they die (11:13). The image of the corpses of the two prophets lying in the street recalls Ezek 11:6. The symbolic naming of Jerusalem as "Sodom and Egypt" reflects oracles against Sodom and Egypt in Ezek 16:26, 48, 53, 56. We have seen that an early Christian prophecy against the temple may be behind Rev 11:2. This section may also draw on such a tradition. Matt 23:29-30 calls the graves of the prophets to witness against Jesus' contemporaries.

The nations that are trampling the holy city are also the ones that will witness the exaltation/resurrection of the two dead prophets. This section preserves a traditional Jewish story pattern: the wicked kill and mock the righteous; the righteous are exalted/resurrected; the wicked see the exalta-tion of those whom they had despised and cry out lamenting their own con-demnation. As with many of the passages in which the author moves toward

be buried. [10]The inhabitants of the earth will gloat over them and be glad and exchange gifts because these two prophets tormented the inhabitants of the earth. [11]But after the three and a half days, a breath of life from God entered them. When they stood on their feet, great fear fell on those who saw them. [12]Then they heard a loud voice from heaven say to them, "Come up here." So they went up to heaven in a cloud as their enemies looked on. [13]At that moment there was a great earthquake, and a tenth of the city fell in ruins. Seven thousand people were killed during the earthquake; the rest were terrified and gave glory to the God of heaven.

[14]The second woe has passed, but the third is coming soon.

The Seventh Trumpet. [15]Then the seventh angel blew his trumpet. There were loud voices in heaven, saying, "The kingdom of the world now belongs to our Lord and to his Anointed, and he will reign forever and ever." [16]The twenty-four elders who sat on their thrones be-

the mythical, Revelation intensifies the grotesque and terrifying in its presentation. Refusal to bury a corpse was the worst punishment antiquity could imagine. An unburied corpse would render the whole city polluted. Yet Revelation shows us people staring at and even celebrating around the two corpses in the street. All the world is involved. The corpses lie there unburied for the symbolic period of three and a half days.

After that period, God acts. The bodies arise as in the dry bones vision of Ezek 37:10 and are carried to heaven like Elijah (2 Kgs 2:11). The earthquake associated with the end of the world was transferred to the crucifixion and resurrection of Christ in Matthew (27:52). The terror of the people watching the sign recalls another Old Testament prophecy which early Christians used for the reaction of the nations when they say the crucified return in glory, Zech 12:10. It is important to remember that in this "exaltation of the righteous" pattern, the wicked acknowledge their sinfulness at the end when they see the righteous person exalted. But that acknowledgment is too late. They are not saved by it. Thus, the nations worship, but they do so out of fear. They are admitting their sinful neglect of the prophetic word. The resurrection/exaltation stands over against the wicked as a sign of their own condemnation.

Verse 14 ties this long section back to the second woe, from which it departed. However, the traditions in these two sections seem to have had an origin in prophecies that were not originally part of the trumpet cycle. We are warned that the final trumpet is about to sound.

11:15-19 The seventh trumpet. We shift back into the focus of the earlier cycles with a vision of the victorious ascent of the Lamb to his throne. Perhaps the early Christian prophecies of resurrection/exaltation and vindication that are related to the images of the previous section help tie that vision to this one. We are lifted out of the terrors of the previous vision to

fore God prostrated themselves and worshiped God [17]and said:

"We give thanks to you, Lord God almighty,

who are and who were.

For you have assumed your great power
and have established your reign.

[18]The nations raged,

but your wrath has come,

and the time for the dead to be
judged,

and to recompense your servants, the
prophets,

and the holy ones and those who fear
your name,

the small and the great alike,

and to destroy those who destroy the
earth."

the heavenly splendor of a new king assuming the throne. The angelic herald announces the beginning of his rule. We are somewhat removed from the woe associated with the seventh trumpet, since the ascent of the Lamb to his throne does not immediately provide the occasion for further destruction on earth.

This vision resumes the earlier vision of the Lamb in chapter 5. That vision concluded with a hymn which proclaims the Lamb worthy to rule (5:9, 12). This one moves beyond that acclamation. The elders are singing a hymn of thanksgiving to the Lamb for having assumed his rule over the nations. That hymn envisages the Lord's rule over the raging nations (Ps 99:1). It proclaims the judgment of those who are hostile to God's people as having occurred. Their sentence has been passed with the enthronement of the Lamb, even though it is clear that the Lord has not yet destroyed such powers from the face of the earth. Jewish legend held that the ark, lost in the destruction of Solomon's temple, would be returned in the messianic age. Here we see it resting within the heavenly temple. The violent storm surrounding the ark is a sign of divine presence.

This vision proclaims the present sovereignty of the Lamb. It provides a heavenly prologue to the horrors of the beast that are to come, much as the visions in chapters 4 and 5 provided a prologue to the first two vision cycles. We are about to move into events which affect the author and his audience. The beast, like the fourth beast from the sea in Daniel, represents the empire under which they live and the imperial ideology against which they must struggle.

UNNUMBERED VISIONS

Rev 12:1–15:4

A new series of visions contrasts the followers of the beast with the followers of the Lamb. Many interpreters think that the dragon's attack on the

¹⁹Then God's temple in heaven was opened, and the ark of his covenant could be seen in the temple. There were flashes of lightning, rumblings, and peals of thunder, an earthquake, and a violent hailstorm.

12 **The Woman and the Dragon.** ¹A great sign appeared in the sky, a woman clothed with the sun, with the moon under her feet, and on her head a crown of twelve stars. ²She was with child and wailed aloud in pain as she labored to give birth. ³Then another sign appeared in the sky; it was a huge red dragon, with seven heads and ten horns, and on its heads were seven diadems. ⁴Its tail swept

woman and her offspring is the third woe. They point to the woe in 12:12: "Woe to you, earth and sea, for the Devil has come down to you in great fury!" The author may also have thought of this section as divided into seven visions. However, he does not provide a numbered cycle for them, and there is no agreement among commentators as to how the section should be divided. All of the literary devices introduced in the first half of the book continue. Horrors on earth alternate with visions of heaven. Symbols loaded with mythological allusions collapse into one another. Present realities and future predictions overlap. We cannot always tell where one begins and another leaves off. The author takes traditional imagery for evil and intensifies it in the direction of the grotesque. However strange these visions may be, we must always remember that they are interpretations of the world that Christians are experiencing. They seek to point out the real truth about the powers at work in that world.

12:1-6 "A woman clothed with the sun." The story of the woman and the dragon draws upon a wealth of symbolism from the myths of the ancient Near East, from Jewish and Greek sources. Many parallels can be brought to the events in this section. We will be content with sketching a few of the major images in order to indicate how deeply rooted the symbol is in the mythic consciousness of humanity. An important function of the woman in Revelation is to provide an antitype to the image of Babylon as whore.

The "woman clothed with the sun" would easily remind the audience of the Roman use of the story of the sun god, Apollo. Roma, the queen of heaven, was worshiped as mother. The emperor Augustus claimed that he had brought about the golden age of kingship associated with Apollo, the sun god. The emperor Nero, who will play a large role in the beast visions to come, went even further. He claimed that as an infant he had been rescued from a serpent's attack just as the infant Apollo had been. The Apollo myth said that Python was seeking to kill Leto, who was pregnant with Apollo, Zeus' son. Zeus has the north wind rescue Leto by carrying her off to an island. Poseidon, the sea god, then contributes to rescuing the woman by covering the island with waves.

away a third of the stars in the sky and hurled them down to the earth. Then the dragon stood before the woman about to give birth, to devour her child when she gave birth. ⁵She gave birth to a son, a male child, destined to rule all the nations with an iron rod. Her child was caught up to God and his throne. ⁶The woman herself fled into the desert where she had a place prepared by God, that there she might be taken care of for twelve hundred and sixty days.

The similarities with the story in Revelation are obvious. The woman clothed with the sun is being pursued by a dragon. She is carried off to safety by an eagle. Then the earth contributes to the rescue by swallowing the dragon's water. Other mythological traditions also tell stories of the goddess-mother who must ward off attack from a serpent being. None of the stories is exactly identical to any of the others, any more than the story in Revelation is the story of Apollo. They all reflect an archetypal symbol of the heavenly mother and her divine child, who are attacked by the evil monster from the waters of chaos. The mother and child must be rescued from the forces of evil.

For the audience of Revelation, which has just seen the enthronement of the Lamb, this scene is a flashback to the primordial story of the birth/rescue of the divine child. It will provide a mythic explanation for the hostility between the followers of the beast and those of the Lamb. It is easy to see why later Christians identified the woman with Mary. However, Revelation stays with the archetypal meaning of the symbol. It does not descend to the level of identification with a single person. All of the images of "the woman" in these chapters are to be read on that transpersonal level. The children of the persecuted woman will also be described as those who must struggle with the dragon on earth. Thus, the sign of the woman in heaven becomes the mythic prototype of the earthly realities that are faced by the audience.

We have already seen that John never takes his images from a single source. The woman also evokes traditions from the Old Testament. Being clothed with the sun recalls the glory with which God, the creator, is clothed in Ps 104:1-2. The twelve stars in her crown have astral symbolism, standing for the twelve signs of the zodiac, but they can also stand for the twelve tribes of Israel (compare the moon and the eleven stars of Joseph's dream in Gen 37:9). Isa 7:14 pointed to the child about to be born as a messianic sign. The woman's labor pains reflect those of the daughter of Zion (Mic 4:10; Isa 26:17). Her cry is reminiscent of the voice calling out from the temple just before Zion gives birth to the Messiah in Isa 66:6-8. The imagery makes it clear that the child born to the woman is the Messiah. He shepherds the nation with a rod of iron (Isa 66:8; 7:14).

⁷Then war broke out in heaven; Michael and his angels battled against the dragon. The dragon and its angels fought back, ⁸but they did not prevail and there was no longer any place for them in heaven. ⁹The huge dragon, the ancient serpent, who is called the Devil and Satan, who deceived the whole world, was

However, we find another of those delays that permeate the images of Revelation. In Isa 66, the woman's birth pangs are followed by the messianic age of salvation. Here they bring on an attack of the dragon, which is still not yet the final showdown between good and evil. The dragon is a mythological representation of the opponent of God. In ancient Near Eastern creation myths, the warrior storm god must conquer the dragon of the watery chaos before the world can be created. In Jewish apocalypses conquest of the beast signals the final destruction of the world and the beginning of the new creation. This beast represents an intensified image of the beast from the sea in Daniel. His color and the destruction of the stars link him with the agents of destruction in the first half of the book. As in Daniel, the beast has many heads to symbolize the many kingdoms (7:7). Stars are swept from the heavens (8:10). As in the trumpet visions, the destruction of the stars is limited to a third.

The dragon is the last of the heavenly signs. The rest of the mythic creatures will emerge from the seas or will be associated with the earth. The symbolic protection of the woman for three and a half years returns at the end of the chapter after the dragon is cast out of heaven. Her flight into the desert recalls the Elijah story (1 Kgs 17:1-7). Presumably, angels care for her in the desert (1 Kgs 19:5-7).

12:7-12 Victory in heaven. We have seen that Revelation consistently shows victories that remain to be won on earth as completed in heaven. The story of Satan's fall from heaven now emerges as a preliminary battle between Michael and Satan. It will show that the persecution and hostility experienced by Christians have their source in this ancient conflict. The myth of the fallen angels has been combined with the imagery of the god's victory over the monster of chaos. The story in Revelation maintains the timeless quality of its mythic symbols. The story of the myth was repeated annually in the cults of the ancient world. It had the quality of being an eternally valid expression of the divine victory over the sources of evil and disorder. Something of those overtones must attach to the heavenly representations of victory in Revelation. Like the myths of old, they would reassure the persecuted of the fundamental victory of order over chaos. Michael is traditionally the guardian of the people of God and the opponent of Satan (see Dan 10:13, 21; 12:1). The heavenly victory symbolizes his permanent dominion over Satanic forces.

thrown down to earth, and its angels were thrown down with it.

¹⁰Then I heard a loud voice in heaven say:
"Now have salvation and power come,
and the kingdom of our God
and the authority of his Anointed.
For the accuser of our brothers is cast out,
who accuses them before our God day and night.
They conquered him by the blood of the Lamb
and by the word of their testimony;
love for life did not deter them from death.

¹² Therefore, rejoice, you heavens, and you who dwell in them.
But woe to you, earth and sea,
for the Devil has come down to you in great fury,
for he knows he has but a short time."

¹³When the dragon saw that it had been thrown down to the earth, it pursued the woman who had given birth to the male child. ¹⁴But the woman was given the two wings of the great eagle, so that she could fly to her place in the desert, where, far from the serpent, she was taken care of for a year, two years, and a half-year. ¹⁵The serpent, however, spewed a torrent

Verse 8 recalls Dan 2:35; verse 9, Isa 14:12. The tradition that Satan's fall from heaven is linked with the messianic age also appears in sayings of Jesus (Luke 10:18; John 12:31). Verse 9 reminds the reader that the dragon being defeated is Satan. The hymn of victory in verses 10-12 sounds an ominous note. On the one hand, it celebrates Michael's victory over Satan and shows that victory to be realized in the victory of God's faithful people. On the other hand, it sounds a note of warning to those on earth.

Casting out of Satan, the heavenly accuser, belongs to the image of the victorious ascent of the Messiah. Satan's attempts to accuse the saints before God have been defeated by their fidelity and by the sacrifice of the Lamb. The jubilation of the hymn reflects Ps 96:10-13 and the rejoicing of the cosmos in Isa 44:23; 49:13. The previous hymns might lead us to expect this hymn to end on that note. Instead, a warning is given. The defeated, angry dragon will be even more severe in his persecution of the woman and her children on earth. Michael's victory has shown that his rule is coming to an end. What follows is a description of the messianic suffering of the faithful rather than of the woes to be visited on the wicked.

12:13-18 The woman's flight. The story of the woman's flight, first exhibited in heaven, is now repeated on earth. Eagle's wings as sign of divine protection appear in the Old Testament (Exod 19:4; Deut 32:11; Isa 40:31). She is cared for again for the symbolic three and a half years. Associated with the waters (see Isa 29:3; Job 40:23), the dragon tries to use his element, raging flood waters, against the woman, but she escapes (Ps 32:6; 69:16). Rescue from raging waters emphasizes the image of the woman as people of God, rescued from the sea and the raging hostility of Pharaoh (Num 16:32; Deut 11:6; Isa 29:3-5, 10; 30:12).

of water out of his mouth after the woman to sweep her away with the current. [16]But the earth helped the woman and opened its mouth and swallowed the flood that the dragon spewed out of its mouth. [17]Then the dragon became angry with the woman and went off to wage war against the rest of her offspring, those who keep God's commandments and bear witness to Jesus. [18]It took its position on the sand of the sea.

13 **The First Beast.** [1]Then I saw a beast come out of the sea with ten horns and seven heads; on its horns were ten diadems, and on its heads blasphemous name[s]. [2]The beast I saw was like a leopard, but it had feet like a bear's, and its mouth was like the mouth of a lion. To it the dragon gave its own power and throne, along with great authority. [3]I saw that one of its heads seemed to have been mortally wounded, but this mortal

Verse 17 makes it clear that the woman stands for the people of God. The dragon goes off to find her offspring. The specification of the righteous as those who "give witness to Jesus" makes the hostility against the Christians the expression of the dragon's anger. However, the author's references to those experiences are indirect, since he continues the practice of imaginative intensification of mythological symbols in this section. Prophetic predictions of salvation, stories of Israel's formation as a people of God, and archaic mythological symbols all blend together in the visions of conflict and salvation that are about to unfold. We have already seen that the letters suggest that many in the audience would not have seen their experience of Roman imperial power as Satanic. Some have probably worked out compromises with the surrounding environment.

13:1-10 The beast from the sea. The dragon's authority comes to rest in two beasts, one from the sea and one from the earth. The beasts symbolize the antichrist and false prophet of the end time in Jewish apocalyptic visions at the same time as they are the final embodiment of imperial power opposed to the rule of God, the final beast of Daniel's visions. We have seen that 4 Ezra pictured Rome as a great eagle emerging from the sea (11, 1). The sea indicates that the beast in question embodies the watery chaos monster of ancient Near Eastern mythology, the primordial source of all evil. The author identifies the beast for his audience by reminding them of a piece of esoteric numerology that would apparently have been well known to Christians in such circumstances: the number of the beast is 666 (13:18). This number is not a prediction of the future. All interpretations of Revelation that claim to attach the number to a present-day figure should be dismissed. This code is one which the author and his audience share. The best solution to the identity of the beast remains "Nero Caesar," since the Hebrew letters for that title add up to 666.

Several other features of Revelation suit the Nero legend and add to our conviction that Nero is the person to whom the author is referring. A legend

wound was healed. Fascinated, the whole world followed after the beast. ⁴They worshiped the dragon because it gave its authority to the beast; they also worshiped the beast and said, "Who can compare with the beast or who can fight against it?"

⁵The beast was given a mouth uttering proud boasts and blasphemies, and it was given authority to act for forty-two months. ⁶It opened its mouth to utter blasphemies against God, blaspheming his name and his dwelling and those who dwell in heaven. ⁷It was also allowed to wage war against the holy ones and conquer them, and it was granted authority over every tribe, people, tongue, and nation. ⁸All the inhabitants of the earth will

circulated among the subject peoples of the eastern part of the empire that Nero had not died. He would return leading a revolt against Rome. Remember the Parthians of the first horseman? The legend held that Nero had fled to live among the Parthians. The period between A.D. 69 and 88 is punctuated by a series of revolts led by those who claimed to be Nero redivivus. We have a collection of Jewish prophecies from this period known as the Jewish Sibylline Oracles. The earlier oracles, from the period after the destruction of the Jerusalem temple by the Romans, picture Nero as leading a great victory of Asian forces over Rome.

In other words, the legend functioned for the Jews at the time much as it did for other conquered peoples in the East: it was a symbol of anti-Roman feeling and hopes for a revolt that would bring freedom and wealth to Asia. Later oracles in the fifth book continue to suggest that Nero is alive somewhere in the East, but they switch their view of Nero to one more like that in Revelation. Nero is identified as the mythological opponent of God in the last days. They make fun of his claims to divine birth. They seem to conceive of Nero as still living and fighting a terrible war against the king sent by God. Other passages both in the Jewish Sibyllines and in a Christian edition of a Jewish apocalypse from the first century, the Ascension of Isaiah, clearly identify Nero with Satan. They speak of him as performing cosmic signs, as claiming to be God, as setting up his image in all the cities and demanding worship from the peoples of the earth. Since Revelation appears to be earlier than all but the oracles in the fourth book of the Jewish Sibyllines, its image of the Satanic Nero may well be the earliest example of the perception that Nero would not return as savior of the eastern peoples but would embody the final outbreak of evil against God and his people.

Remember, most people seem to have thought that Nero was still alive, even though he was said to have died. That was not difficult to believe, since he had only been about thirty-one at the time of his death. Verse 3 describes a mortal wound on the head of the beast, which nonetheless lives. The story of Nero's coming from the East with Parthian troops seems to be referred to in 17:8-10, when the author speaks of the amazement of the peoples who worship it, all whose names were not written from the foundation of the world in the book of life, which belongs to the Lamb who was slain.

⁹Whoever has ears ought to hear these words.

¹⁰Anyone destined for captivity goes into captivity.
Anyone destined to be slain by the sword shall be slain by the sword.

Such is the faithful endurance of the holy ones.

see the beast who once existed, now does not exist, and will exist again. We have already seen that the image of the woman with the sun in chapter 12 serves as an antithesis to the imperial propaganda which pictured Nero in terms of the Apollo legend. Finally, the emperor who appears to have been on the throne at the time Revelation was composed also tried to appropriate the positive side of the Nero image. He used "Nero Caesar" as one of his official titles.

Considering the positive expectations of Nero in the populace at large, it was necessary to speak in a symbolic and guarded way. Criticism of Roman rule was dangerous to begin with. Revelation adds to that critique the presentation of Nero, a symbol of reversal for many opposed to that rule, that makes him the epitome of Rome's demonic power. At the same time, symbolic words about and allusions to Nero and the political affairs of the region were a common way of speaking. Both Jews and Christians would understand the type of writing embodied in the prophecies of Revelation. The author has not tried to conceal his meaning from those who are accustomed to such a way of speaking.

The two beasts, sea and land, have their counterparts in Behemoth and Leviathan of Job 40:15-27. They also reflect the beast of the final empire in Dan 7:3. Daniel divides world history into four empires, each represented by a beast and each hostile to God. Revelation is following a tactic that it used before when it compresses the four beasts into one and intensifies the grotesque nature of the beast by adding heads. The audience would have no trouble recognizing that the beast represented the empire of their experience, the Roman Empire. They would see the challenge to the Roman Empire's claim to enjoy the favor of the gods and even be ruled by a "divine" emperor in the picture of the beast as the embodiment of Satan. In addition to Jewish and Christian apocalypses, there is some evidence for "apocalyptic" thought among the conquered peoples of Egypt and Babylonia. Though the mortal conflict between the sovereignty of a "Satan" and the true God is not necessarily part of pagan apocalypses, they show a longing for national liberation, return to tradition, and to former glory that is much like the desires of their Jewish counterparts. The general development of eschatological expectations among peoples of the East after the conquests of Alexander the Great has been understood by some political philosophers as evidence of the "underside" of imperial conquest. The self-glorifying and even self-divinizing inscriptions and proclamations of the imperial rulers presented the empire as beneficent. So does the literature written by those who benefited from the opportunities given by imperial expansion. We have seen that those local, civic authorities who sought favor with the empire joined the proclamation of the benefits of the empire through the various cultic activities in honor of the emperor. Clearly, the local citizenry did not have a universally agreed upon assessment of the empire.

Indeed, Revelation portrays most of the world as awed by the beast. None could imagine that its power would be overthrown. Just as the beast is a double parody of both the emperor and the false messiah, the antichrist, so following the beast is not just a sign of loyalty to the empire. It is also a parody of true Christian discipleship. The wound which heals not only refers to the legends about Nero. It also parodies the true healing of mortality in the resurrection, Christ, who died and now lives. The two witnesses lifted up into heaven in chapter 11 can also be seen as the antitype of another imperial symbol, the apotheosis of the emperor. Art works represent the deceased emperor being carried up to the heavens to be with the gods. Some people even claimed to have seen the souls of deceased emperors ascending into heaven from their funeral pyres. Such false claims of imperial divinity contribute to the veneration of the emperor. Revelation has already shown its audience that the true exaltation is Christ's ascent to the throne from which he now rules. The acclamation which the peoples give the beast are a parody of the true hymns of praise that are sung in heaven to the Lamb. Verse 4 even parodies the celebration of God's triumph over his enemies in Exod 15:11. The audience already knows from the previous battle in heaven that Michael, the heavenly angels, and even God's faithful ones can triumph over this beast which the world holds in such awe. The audience knows the answer to that rhetorical question, "Who can compare with the beast or who can come forward to fight against it?"

Verses 5-8 intensify the conflict imagery. The symbolic forty-two-month period represents the time of authority given any hostile power. Some interpreters suggest that the blasphemy referred to in verse 6 belongs to the titles of Domitian, the ruling emperor. He was called "dominus et deus," lord and god. These verses make it clear that the world itself is divided in two between the followers of the beast and the followers of the Lamb. Only those who belong to the Lamb will hold out against the dominion of the beast.

The story of the first beast ends with a prophetic oracle. The familiar call to hear suggests that it is directed to the followers of the Lamb and is not a woe oracle against the followers of the beast. The first part reflects

The Second Beast. [11]Then I saw another beast come up out of the earth; it had two horns like a lamb's but spoke like a dragon. [12]It wielded all the authority of the first beast in its sight and made the earth and its inhabitants worship the first beast, whose mortal wound had been healed. [13]It performed great signs, even making fire come down from heaven to earth in the sight of everyone. [14]It deceived the inhabitants of the earth with the signs it was allowed to perform in the sight of the first beast, telling them to make an image for the beast who had been wounded by the sword and revived. [15]It was then permitted to breathe life into

Jer 15:2. The oracle may also be related to Matt 26:5. The oracle clearly warns the faithful of a period of suffering. Perhaps it also intends to instruct them that no human revolt will stop its blasphemy. Some interpreters point to the Jewish rebellion under Trajan about twenty years later as evidence that such warnings were in order. Revelation may also have an earlier Christian oracle from the time of the Jewish revolt in A.D. 66–70 in mind.

13:11-18 The beast from the land. The authority of the first beast is passed to a second. However, both beasts clearly represent the empire. Verse 12 suggests that the second beast represents the power of the empire as it was exercised by local authorities. We have already seen that the spread of the emperor cult in the East was due to the initiatives of local governments and private citizens. They usually thought to gain some imperial favor or recognition for their city. Verse 12 describes such a process at the same time that it hints once again that the beast is Nero. We have seen that the signs and wonders could belong to the Nero legend. However, they are also typical of the false prophets of the end time (see Matt 24:24). Calling down fire from heaven was considered a particularly impressive sign of divine power (see 1 Kgs 18:21-23 and the disciples' request of Jesus in Luke 9:51-56). Cities and temples might also claim signs and miracles as a way of gaining support for local shrines. The cultic imagery continues in verse 14 when the people are instructed to erect a cult statue. Failure to worship will carry a death penalty (compare Dan 3:2-3). We have no evidence for any attempt to enforce such veneration throughout the empire. Pliny's correspondence with Trajan two decades later shows that the Romans had no specific crime with which to charge those denounced as Christians. Pliny and Trajan are willing to dismiss those accused of being Christians if they will acknowledge imperial power by offering incense before a statue of the emperor. They also refuse to accept anonymous accusations against people. Should the accused comply with the imperial directive, the person who brought the charge would have to pay a penalty. Should the accused resist, he or she would be executed as a potential danger to the state. We do not know how such cases were handled in Asia Minor at the time of Revelation. Perhaps such prob-

the beast's image, so that the beast's image could speak and [could] have anyone who did not worship it put to death. [16]It forced all the people, small and great, rich and poor, free and slave, to be given a stamped image on their right hands or their foreheads, [17]so that no one could buy or sell except one who had the stamped image of the beast's name or the number that stood for its name.

[18]Wisdom is needed here; one who understands can calculate the number of the beast, for it is a number that stands for a person. His number is six hundred and sixty-six.

14 The Lamb's Companions. [1]Then I looked and there was the Lamb standing on Mount Zion, and with him a hundred and forty-four thousand who had his name and his Father's name written on their foreheads. [2]I heard a sound from heaven like the sound of rushing water or a loud peal of thunder. The sound I heard was like that of harpists

lems are only beginning and John is warning Christians that the beast will eventually expand its demands.

We have no direct evidence for a practice of marking people on the forehead such as we find mentioned in verse 16. John may have created that image as an antitype to the sealing of Christian baptism. The "sign" which a person wears identifies him or her as a member of either the followers of the beast or the followers of the Lamb. There is no grey area in between. Verse 17 rapidly brings us back to the sober reality of refusing to comply with demands to venerate the emperor. Christians seem to be excluded from or at a disadvantage in commerce, an important activity in cities like Laodicea. The letter to that city certainly hints that Christians were as much involved in its commercial prosperity as any of the other citizens. Some interpreters think that the disadvantage came from a refusal to use coins, which often carried images of the emperor as divine on one side. However, even if Christians did use such coins, they might still face problems. They might refuse to swear oaths that accompanied many transactions if they mentioned the emperor as divine. Thus it would appear difficult for Christians to engage in commercial transactions with non-Christians without being willing to go along with customs which appeared to acknowledge the divinity and authority of the beast.

14:1-5 The followers of the Lamb. The scene now shifts back to the 144,000, those who bear the mark of the Lamb. Condemnation of imperial power will resume in chapter 17. Mount Zion was often pictured as the place where the Messiah would appear prior to his final battle with the forces of evil. Here the Lamb appears with his faithful ones. This image consolidates the opposition between the two groups, the followers of the beast and the followers of the Lamb. This group is described as the "first fruit" of the people of God. Verse 16:14 will show the gathering together of the nations at the end time.

playing their harps. ³They were singing [what seemed to be] a new hymn before the throne, before the four living creatures and the elders. No one could learn this hymn except the hundred and forty-four thousand who had been ransomed from the earth. ⁴These are they who were not defiled with women; they are virgins and these are the one who follow the Lamb wherever he goes. They have been ransomed as the firstfruits of the human race for God and the Lamb. ⁵On their lips no deceit has been found; they are unblemished.

The Three Angels. ⁶Then I saw another angel flying high overhead, with everlasting good news to announce to those who dwell on earth, to every nation, tribe, tongue, and people. ⁷He said in a loud voice, "Fear God and give him glory, for his time has come to sit in judgment. Worship him who made heaven and earth and sea and springs of water."

⁸A second angel followed, saying:
"Fallen, fallen is Babylon the great,
    that made all the nations drink
    the wine of her licentious passion."

The opening of this scene recalls prophetic announcements of the day of Yahweh (see Joel 2:27; 3:3-5). However, this gathering is not the end. Instead, we are given the antitype to the worship paid to the beast. The 144,000 learn the "new hymn" to be sung before the Lamb. Revelation sees the prophetic promises that the remnant of Israel will be purified and will dwell without sin on God's holy mountain as fulfilled in this group (Zeph 3:8-13; Isa 53:9). Perfection and holiness are characteristics of the true people of God redeemed by the Lamb. Since Christians are being warned against the idolatry of worshiping the beast, we find the customary assertions of sexual purity in the assertion that the followers of the Lamb "were not defiled with women." This verse does not mean that Christians were expected to be ascetics. Jewish prophetic language often spoke of idolatry as sexual immorality. Revelation will come back to this combination in the pictures of the whore of Babylon in chapter 17. The angel is about to announce the destruction of Babylon (14:8).

14:6-13 Announcements of judgment. Remember the three cries of woe from the eagle in midheaven (8:13)? Now an angelic herald flies across midheaven calling out oracles of divine judgment. These oracles warn against following the beast. At the same time as the announcement of divine judgment means woe for those who follow the beast, it represents salvation for the faithful. It summons them to repentance and endurance. Consequently, the first angel is pictured as proclaiming the "gospel," the eternal good news, to all the people on earth. The gospel message given by the angel is that the time of salvation is at hand; the creator of heaven and earth has assumed his throne. Thus, the hymns in other parts of Revelation which celebrate the victory of the Lamb are also announcements of the gospel according to Revelation. The announcement recalls the celebration of the victory of the

⁹A third angel followed them and said in a loud voice, "Anyone who worships the beast or its image, or accepts its mark on forehead or hand, ¹⁰will also drink the wine of God's fury, poured full strength into the cup of his wrath, and will be tormented in burning sulfur before the holy angels and before the Lamb. ¹¹The smoke of the fire that torments them will rise forever and ever, and there will be no relief day or night for those who worship the beast or its image or accept the mark of its name." ¹²Here is what sustains the holy ones who keep God's commandments and their faith in Jesus.

¹³I heard a voice from heaven say, "Write this: Blessed are the dead who die in the Lord from now on." "Yes," said the Spirit, "let them find rest from their labors, for their works accompany them."

The Harvest of the Earth. ¹⁴Then I looked and there was a white cloud, and sitting on the cloud one who looked like a son of man, with a gold crown on his

Lord on his holy mountain in Isa 25:9-10. The angel in Revelation is summoning the whole world to pay homage to its victorious creator.

The second angel brings an oracle of woe against Babylon which combines Isa 21:9 and Jer 59:7. Jewish apocalypses always identify the ruling empire with the Babylonian Empire, so that in Daniel, Babylon is the Syrian Empire of Alexander's successors. Revelation, of course, identifies Rome and Babylon. Once again, drinking the "wine of her lewdness" refers to homage and idolatry. These images will be expanded in the vision of Babylon, the great.

The third angel concludes with a stern warning against worshiping the beast. The punishments combine a number of prophetic themes. Sinners drink the cup of divine wrath (Isa 51:17, 22; Jer 25:15). They experience the sulphur sent on Sodom and find themselves in everlasting torment (Isa 66:24; 34:9f.). The godless have no rest (Ps 95:11). Their torment contrasts with the peace which awaits the faithful (Isa 57:2, 10).

Verses 12 and 13 apply these oracles to the followers of the Lamb. They are encouraged to persevere. They are promised that their fate will not be like the death of those who worship the beast. Remember, all these cries of woe are not invitations for Christians to gloat over the eventual fate of their enemies. They are reassurance for those who might be tempted to give up, who might think that the "gospel" of God's rule over the world just couldn't be true, who might be in awe of the greatness and power of the beast themselves. Revelation uses all the symbolic resources at its disposal to show that God's salvation is the truth about power and dominion for all the nations of the world, that it really does matter whether or not one resists the power of the beast.

14:14-20 The eschatological harvest. This image of the angelic harvest of the earth combines two Old Testament passages, Dan 7:13 and Joel 4:13-16. The harvest takes place in two stages: first wheat, then grapes. The image

head and a sharp sickle in his hand. [15]Another angel came out of the temple, crying out in a loud voice to the one sitting on the cloud, "Use your sickle and reap the harvest, for the time to reap has come, because the earth's harvest is fully ripe." [16]So the one who was sitting on the cloud swung his sickle over the earth, and the earth was harvested.

[17]Then another angel came out of the temple in heaven who also had a sharp sickle. [18]Then another angel [came] from the altar, [who] was in charge of the fire, and cried out in a loud voice to the one who had the sharp sickle, "Use your sharp sickle and cut the clusters from the earth's vines, for its grapes are ripe." [19]So the angel swung his sickle over the earth and cut the earth's vintage. He threw it into the great wine press of God's fury. [20]The wine press was trodden outside the city and blood poured out of the wine press to the height of a horse's bridle for two hundred miles.

of the Son of Man on the clouds is taken from Dan 7:13. Although early Christians usually applied the Son of Man image to the second coming of Jesus, the Son of Man here is an angel. He is subject to the command of another angelic voice from the temple. We have seen that pattern frequently in the earlier scenes of angelic workers of destruction. The first harvest recalls the saying about the lord of the harvest in Mark 4:29 and the angelic reapers of Matt 13:39. Opinion on the significance of the first harvest is divided. Some scholars see it as the destruction of the pagan nations that come to attack the Messiah on his holy mountain in the last days. Others point to the positive images of the wheat harvest elsewhere in the New Testament. They suggest that the first act of harvesting gathers the righteous prior to the judgment of the wicked. We favor the first opinion. Joel 4:13-16 gives the basic elements of this vision. The call to harvest with sickle and winepress is negative. After the harvest oracle, the prophet proclaims the holiness and salvation of the Lord's people on Mount Zion. Revelation has presented us with the elements of this prophecy in reverse order. We have seen the vision of the holy ones on Mount Zion (14:1-5). They have been promised that the Lord is coming in judgment (14:7). Now that harvest begins.

There is no question about the negative imagery attached to the grape harvest in the second half of the passage. The angel at the incense altar ties this vision back to the earlier visions of the trumpets. Before the trumpets began, he brought the prayers of the holy ones to God and then cast the coals from the censer down on the earth (8:3-4). Then he commanded the angel of the sixth trumpet to release the deadly horsemen from the banks of the Euphrates to kill a third of humanity (9:13). Now we find a third grim reminder of the deadly consequences of that angel's voice as he unleashes the trampling of the grapes of wrath. Verse 18 recalls Jer 25:30. Trampling the enemies of God in a great winepress was traditional (see Isa 63:1-6). The enemies of God are turned into a great sea of blood.

15 **The Seven Last Plagues.** [1]Then I saw in heaven another sign, great and awe-inspiring: seven angels with the seven last plagues, for through them God's fury is accomplished.

[2]Then I saw something like a sea of glass mingled with fire. On the sea of glass were standing those who had won the victory over the beast and its image and the number that signified its name. They were holding God's harps, [3]and they sang the song of Moses, the servant of God, and the song of the Lamb:

"Great and wonderful are your works,
  Lord God almighty.
Just and true are your ways,
  O king of the nations.
[4]Who will not fear you, Lord,
  or glorify your name?
For you alone are holy.
  All the nations will come
  and worship before you,
  for your righteous acts have been revealed."

[5]After this I had another vision. The temple that is the heavenly tent of testi-

15:1-4 The song of Moses. Once again, just as we feel the narrative coming close to the great day of divine wrath and judgment, Revelation turns away. Verse 1 announces the final plagues, but they are interrupted by the song of the victors. Many interpreters think that the final woe, announced by the trumpets and then delayed, is represented in the vision of destruction that comes with the last cycle of seven—the seven bowls. In the interlude, we return once again to the heavenly temple. The images of the sea of the beast and the sea of blood are reversed in this image of a sea of glass and fire on which the victors over the beast stand to sing their hymn. The "song of Moses" and "of the Lamb" praises God and promises that all the nations of the earth will come to worship the Lord when they see his mighty deeds. It appears to be a collage of Old Testament passages (see Pss 111:2; 139:14; Amos 4:13; Jer 10:7; Pss 145:17; 86:9; Hos 6:5). This song looks forward to the universal recognition of God's rule which has been the theme emphasized again and again by the scenes of heavenly praise.

THE SEVEN BOWLS

Rev 15:5–16:21

This cycle brings to a conclusion the series of plagues on earth. Each of the cycles has repeated the theme of the coming judgment from a different perspective. Each has been more intense than the previous one. Each opens with a series of short plagues and concludes with more elaborate and mythological ones at the end. Like the trumpet cycle, the bowl plagues include allusions to the Exodus plagues. The image of the bowl combines two elements from the Old Testament traditions that have already been presented in the course of Revelation. Exod 27:3 describes the bronze basins used by the priest

mony opened, ⁶and the seven angels with the seven plagues came out of the temple. They were dressed in clean white linen, with a gold sash around their chests. ⁷One of the four living creatures gave the seven angels seven gold bowls filled with the fury of God, who lives forever and ever. ⁸Then the temple became so filled with the smoke from God's glory and might that no one could enter it until the seven plagues of the seven angels had been accomplished.

16 **The Seven Bowls.** ¹I heard a loud voice speaking from the temple to the seven angels, "Go and pour out the seven bowls of God's fury upon the earth."

²The first angel went and poured out his bowl on the earth. Festering and ugly sores broke out on those who had the mark of the beast or worshiped its image.

³The second angel poured out his bowl on the sea. The sea turned to blood like that from a corpse; every creature living in the sea died.

⁴The third angel poured out his bowl on the rivers and springs of water. These also turned to blood. ⁵Then I heard the angel in charge of the waters say:

"You are just, O Holy One,

to carry out the ashes and fat from the sacrifices. Rev 8:3-5 has the angel at the altar of incense empty the censer of coals on the earth. Here, angels come out of the temple carrying bowls filled with the plagues. The second image, introduced in the vision of the winepress, is that of the cup of wine, which represents the wrath of God (Ps 75:8; Isa 51:17, 22). Also, like the previous plagues, these plagues do not bring people to worship God or to repent. They only continue to blaspheme the Lord, thus sealing their own doom.

15:5-8 The angels carry out bowls of wrath. Chapters 9 and 10 of Ezekiel provide the model for this section. In that section of Ezekiel, the scribe and six angels make up the needed seven. They are summoned to execute the guilty ones in the city of God. The scribe goes before the angels and marks the righteous to spare them from destruction. Revelation does not need such a process, since the righteous and the wicked already bear the seal of the one whom they follow. The description of the angels combines Dan 10:5-6 and Ezek 28:5. Ezek 10:4 describes the cloud of divine glory which fills the temple when the Lord is present. Here the smoke symbolic of his presence prohibits anyone from entering the temple until the plagues are carried out. In Ezek 10:6-8 the angels cast fire on the earth from the divine throne chariot. Here one of the chariot creatures gives the bowls to the angels.

16:1-11 The first five plagues. The first five plagues strike humans and water creatures with sores, blood, fire, and darkness. The voice which calls out from the temple may be that of God (see Isa 66:6), since no one can enter there, or that of the revealing angel (see Ezek 9:1). The intensification of these plagues is indicated by the affliction which hits the whole earth, not just a part of it. The third plague, which destroys all fresh drinking water, is accompanied by an antiphonal proclamation of the justice of God's judgment

who are and who were,
in passing this sentence.
⁶For they have shed the blood of the holy
ones and the prophets,
and you [have] given them blood to
drink;
it is what they deserve."
⁷Then I heard the altar cry out,
"Yes, Lord God almighty,
your judgments are true and just."
⁸The fourth angel poured out his bowl on
the sun. It was given the power to burn
people with fire. ⁹People were burned by
the scorching heat and blasphemed the
name of God who had power over these
plagues, but they did not repent or give
him glory.
¹⁰The fifth angel poured out his bowl
on the throne of the beast. Its kingdom
was plunged into darkness, and people bit
their tongues in pain ¹¹and blasphemed
the God of heaven because of their pains
and sores. But they did not repent of their
works.
¹²The sixth angel emptied his bowl on
the great river Euphrates. Its water was
dried up to prepare the way for the kings
of the East. ¹³I saw three unclean spirits
like frogs come from the mouth of the
dragon, from the mouth of the beast, and

against those who have shed the blood of the righteous (see Pss 119:137; 145:17; 79:3; Isa 49:26). The fourth plague combines the apocalyptic sign in the sun with the casting of fire on the earth. Instead of darkening, as in other apocalyptic visions like the third trumpet, the sun flares up and burns people with its fire. The darkness of the final plague resembles the darkness over Egypt. It also recalls the destruction of the light of the heavenly bodies in the earlier plagues. Human suffering comes from the affliction with boils, as in the first plague of this series.

The fourth and fifth plagues are also linked to the earlier trumpet series in their emphasis on humanity's failure to repent. Instead of turning from wickedness, humans blaspheme God all the more as the cause of their suffering. This intensification of their hostility to God prepares the way for the summoning of destruction from the East. In Isa 46:11-13, Yahweh answers the hard of heart by summoning his man from the East. That summons is the prelude to salvation: the beautiful daughter of Babylon is reduced from luxury to slavery in Isa 47. Revelation will follow a similar pattern. We are about to see the luxurious daughter of Babylon and then to witness her fall. However, two more plagues intervene before we come to that vision.

16:12-16 Armies assemble in the East. We have already seen that people expected destruction from the Parthians in the East. We have also seen that Revelation turns to more grotesque and mythological images for the concluding plagues of a series. The sixth plague presents us with a ghastly image of the armies drawing up for battle. In a mockery of "preparing the way of the Lord," the river Euphrates is dried up to provide a way for the demonic armies. Like the Egyptian frogs (Exod 7:6-11; Pss 7:45; 105:30), they come forth. They work signs and assemble all the kings of the earth for battle.

from the mouth of the false prophet. ¹⁴These were demonic spirits who performed signs. They went out to the kings of the whole world to assemble them for the battle on the great day of God the almighty. ¹⁵("Behold, I am coming like a thief." Blessed is the one who watches and keeps his clothes ready, so that he may not go naked and people see him exposed.) ¹⁶They then assembled the kings in the place that is named Armageddon in Hebrew.

¹⁷The seventh angel poured out his bowl in the air. A loud voice came out of the temple from the throne, saying, "It is done." ¹⁸Then there were lightning flashes, rumblings, and peals of thunder, and a great earthquake. It was such a violent earthquake that there has never been one like it since the human race began on earth. ¹⁹The great city was split into three parts, and the gentile cities fell. But God remembered great Babylon, giving it the cup filled with the wine of his fury and wrath. ²⁰Every island fled, and mountains disappeared. ²¹Large hailstones like huge weights came down from the sky on people, and they blasphemed God for the plague of hail because this plague was so severe.

This assembling provides a demonic antitype for the assembling of the righteous with the Lamb in chapter 14. It translates into the macabre imagery of Revelation—the prophetic vision of the armies coming against Jerusalem in Zech 14:2-5. Zechariah shows us the Lord going forth against his enemies from Zion. When he stands on the Mount of Olives, it splits in two; the valley fills and a great earthquake ensues. Later in the same vision, the Lord strikes his enemies with a plague that causes their flesh to rot (Zech 14:12).

Verse 15 interrupts these predictions of disaster with warnings to the righteous to be on their guard. Related sayings about the second coming are common in the New Testament (see Matt 24:43; Luke 12:39; 1 Thess 5:2, 4; 2 Pet 3:10).

16:17-21 The seventh bowl. We have seen that the violent earthquake, lightning flashes, and announcement of judgment with "it is done" all belong to the scenario for the appearance of God at the end of the world. That theophany should, as in Zech 14, bring the final destruction of the wicked. Once again we will be put off. The description of Babylon and her destruction is being held off until the next section.

The final plague is ordered from the throne in the sanctuary and is accompanied by all the signs of a theophany. The division of the great city and its fall may have been derived from the image of the quake on the Mount of Olives. Revelation is recapitulating the woe of 14:3-16 and looking forward to the vision of the fall of the "great city" Babylon which is to come in the next section of the work. Flight of the islands and mountains is a sign of the divine appearance (see Isa 41:5). Even the destruction of a multitude of cities and great hailstones do nothing to change the ways of humanity. As they have done in response to the earlier plagues, they continue to blas-

V: THE PUNISHMENT OF BABYLON AND THE DESTRUCTION OF PAGAN NATIONS

17 **Babylon the Great.** ¹Then one of the seven angels who were holding the seven bowls came and said to me, "Come here. I will show you the judgment on the great harlot who lives near the many waters. ²The kings of the earth have had intercourse with her, and the inhabitants of the earth became drunk on the wine of her harlotry." ³Then he carried me away in spirit to a deserted place where I saw a woman seated on a scarlet beast that was covered with blasphemous names, with seven heads and ten horns. ⁴The woman was wearing purple and scarlet and adorned with gold, precious stones, and pearls. She held in her hand a gold cup that was filled with the abominable and sordid deeds of her

pheme. The evil of the last days is intensified by the punishments which God has sent against humanity.

BABYLON THE GREAT

Rev 17:1-19:10

All the delay and expectation, all the hints of the fall of Babylon will come to a head in this section. Her fall was announced in 14:8. Chapter 18 will finally show us her demise. First, a description of her appearance reminds the reader that Babylon represents the Satanic power of imperial Rome.

17:1-6 The great whore of Babylon. One of the bowl angels takes the seer to witness the destruction of Babylon. The seventh bowl identified Jerusalem as city of destruction with Babylon. The epithet "harlot" recalls the prophetic oracles against a faithless Jerusalem as well as against other cities (see Isa 1:21; 23:15-18; Ezek 16:15-35; 23:3-49). The drunkenness of the kings of the earth appears in Jer 25:15-29. There it is the cup of wrath from the hand of the Lord which is given to the nations.

There is no direct Old Testament image for the harlot riding on the beast. However, John may have created the image out of chapter 13 and pagan cultic imagery. The color of the beast reminds us of all the plagues of blood and fire that have been shed on the earth throughout the book. The interpretation in the second half of the chapter makes it clear that this vision is a variant of the earlier vision of the beast. The description of the woman combines several Old Testament images from Isa 3:16-24 against the finery of the daughters of Zion; Ezek 28:11-16 against the wealth and ostentation of Tyre; and Jer 51:7 against Babylon. In Jer 51:7, Babylon is the golden cup in the hand of the Lord which makes the nations drunk. Here they are drunk with the lewdness of the harlot (=idolatry) just as the beast was leading the world into idolatry in chapter 13.

harlotry. [5]On her forehead was written a name, which is a mystery, "Babylon the great, the mother of harlots and of the abominations of the earth." [6]I saw that the woman was drunk on the blood of the holy ones and on the blood of the witnesses to Jesus.

Meaning of the Beast and Harlot. When I saw her I was greatly amazed. [7]The angel said to me, "Why are you amazed? I will explain to you the mystery of the woman and of the beast that carries her, the beast with the seven heads and the ten horns. [8]The beast that you saw existed once but now exists no longer. It will come up from the abyss and is headed for destruction. The inhabitants of the earth whose names have not been written in the book of life from the foundation of the world shall be amazed when they see the beast, because it existed once but exists no longer, and yet it will come again. [9]Here is a clue for one who has wisdom. The seven heads represent seven hills upon which the woman sits. They also represent seven kings: [10]five have already fallen, one still lives, and the last has not yet come, and when he comes he must remain only a short while. [11]The beast that existed once but exists no longer is an eighth king, but really belongs to the seven and is headed for destruction. [12]The ten horns that you saw represent ten kings who have not yet been

The symbolic name on the forehead of the harlot recalls the other names which the faithful, whose blood she drinks, have received; the mark of the beast on the forehead of its followers, points to the seal on the foreheads of those who follow the Lamb (9:2). She is drunk with the blood of those faithful ones (16:16; 18:24; cf. the image of the land drunk with blood in Isa 34:7). The faithful martyrs reappear at the end of this section.

17:7-18 Interpretation of the vision of the whore. Like the earlier picture of the beast, this one is a symbolic expansion of traditional imagery. Like most symbolic accounts of history, the number of heads does not match a strictly historical account of the Roman emperors. It seems to best represent a rough sketch of the emperors up to the time of Domitian. Clearly, the beast that returns as the eighth, but is one of the seven, refers to Nero. The eagle vision of the Roman Empire in 4 Ezra has wings which may intend to represent all the emperors, but it only selects three to represent the heads: Vespasian, Titus, Domitian (11:29-32; 12:22-28). The best suggestion is that the emperors indicated represent those particularly hated. Since Revelation is close to contemporary Jewish apocalypses in its anti-Roman sentiment, we may use those sources to suggest a possible identification.

Caligula was the first emperor to cause opposition among the Jews when he demanded that his statue be set up in the temple. (Remember, the beast is accused of doing that in Rev 13:15.) Beginning with Caligula, the heads would represent Caligula, Claudius, Nero, Vespasian, and Titus. Domitian, "the one who is," is sixth. One further emperor is needed to fill out the number seven. As in many apocalypses, the author feels that he is almost but not quite in the last days. The rule of the seventh emperor is to be very short.

crowned; they will receive royal authority along with the beast for one hour. [13]They are of one mind and will give their power and authority to the beast. [14]They will fight with the Lamb, but the Lamb will conquer them, for he is Lord of lords and king of kings, and those with him are called, chosen, and faithful."

[15]Then he said to me, "The waters that you saw where the harlot lives represent large numbers of peoples, nations, and tongues. [16]The ten horns that you saw and the beast will hate the harlot; they will leave her desolate and naked; they will eat her flesh and consume her with fire. [17]For God has put it into their minds to carry out his purpose and to make them come to an agreement to give their kingdom to the beast until the words of God are accomplished. [18]The woman whom you saw represents the great city that has sovereignty over the kings of the earth."

18 **The Fall of Babylon.** [1]After this I saw another angel coming down from heaven, having great authority, and

No one can miss the parallel between the beast and Rome, since the woman is enthroned on the seven hills of that city. Verse 11 associates the coming of the eschatological age with Nero's return from the East. The ten horns are taken from the vision in Dan 7:7, 27. They appear to represent allies of Rome, who suddenly bring the destruction of the harlot by turning viciously against her. Although Revelation uses more archaic and bizarre imagery than the Old Testament prophets, the author shares their conviction that the nations of the world finally do the Lord's bidding. He can turn the nations from friendship to hatred when that is necessary to the plan of salvation. Though the horns hint at the destruction of the harlot by the victorious Lamb and the revolt of her own allies, the full description of her fall awaits the next scene. Verse 16 alludes to a number of prophetic texts (Hos 2:4; Ezek 23:29; Jer 41:42; Mic 3:3).

This interpretation of the harlot vision repeats much of what the audience has already heard. The whole world is taken in by the beast except the followers of the Lamb. They have the insight and wisdom to know the truth about the times in which they live. They can identify the harlot as Rome and know the fate which awaits her. They are not taken in by her pretensions to divinity. The title of the beast, "existed once but exists no longer, and yet it will come again" (v. 8), may even be a parody of the title of God, "who is and who was and who is to come," from the opening of Revelation (1:4). They are certain of their salvation, since their names are recorded in the book of life (see Dan 12:1).

18:1-8 Fallen, fallen is Babylon. Rev 14:8 announced the fall of Babylon. Now a great angel from heaven announces that the condemnation passed by the heavenly court is upon her. This angel is more glorious than all the others we have seen (compare Ezek 43:2). Dan 4:27 provides the epithet "Babylon the great." Several Old Testament prophetic oracles against great

the earth became illumined by his splendor. ²He cried out in a mighty voice:

"Fallen, fallen is Babylon the great.
  She has become a haunt for demons.
She is a cage for every unclean spirit,
  a cage for every unclean bird,
  [a cage for every unclean] and disgusting [beast].
³For all the nations have drunk
  the wine of her licentious passion.
The kings of the earth had intercourse with her,
  and the merchants of the earth grew rich from her drive for luxury."

⁴Then I heard another voice from heaven say:

"Depart from her, my people,
  so as not to take part in her sins
  and receive a share in her plagues,
⁵for her sins are piled up to the sky,
  and God remembers her crimes.

⁶Pay her back as she has paid others.
  Pay her back double for her deeds.
  Into her cup pour double what she poured.
⁷To the measure of her boasting and wantonness
  repay her in torment and grief;
for she said to herself,
  'I sit enthroned as queen;
  I am no widow,
  and I will never know grief.'
⁸Therefore, her plagues will come in one day,
  pestilence, grief, and famine;
  she will be consumed by fire.
For mighty is the Lord God who judges her."

⁹The kings of the earth who had intercourse with her in their wantonness will weep and mourn over her when they see the smoke of her pyre. ¹⁰They will keep

cities are recalled in this passage (see Isa 13:21; 34:11, 14; Jer 50:39; 51:8). This passage comes closest to the condemnation of Tyre in Ezek 27:12-18. Nah 3:3-4 describes Babylon as a city of prostitution and drunkenness. Isa 23:17 refers to the drunkenness of the pagan nations. However, the oracles against Tyre bring out the theme of a city whose luxuries are due to trade and whose fall is not prevented by that great wealth.

The two angelic voices present the grounds for the condemnation of Babylon. When she is sentenced for her crimes, God will repay her double for all the evil she has done. The righteous are warned to flee Babylon, lest they become entangled in her sins. Similar warnings occur in the oracles against Babylon in Jer 50 and 51. Other passages from Jeremiah and Isaiah provide the pattern for the rest of the second announcement. Verse 5 is modeled on Jer 51:9; verse 6, on Jer 51:15, 29 (also Isa 40:2). Verses 7-8 reflect Isa 47:1-9. But while Isaiah tells the boastful daughter of Babylon that she will suffer both loss of husband and loss of children in a single day, Revelation tells her that she will suffer all the plagues, death, mourning, famine, being consumed by fire, at once. The punishment of this Babylon will epitomize all the plagues described in the book at one time.

18:9-10 The kings of the earth lament. Those who had profited by the prosperity and sinfulness of the city now lament her fate. The inspiration

their distance for fear of the torment inflicted on her, and they will say:

"Alas, alas, great city,
    Babylon, mighty city.
    In one hour your judgment has come."

[11]The merchants of the earth will weep and mourn for her, because there will be no more markets for their cargo: [12]their cargo of gold, silver, precious stones, and pearls; fine linen, purple silk, and scarlet cloth; fragrant wood of every kind, all articles of ivory and all articles of the most expensive wood, bronze, iron, and marble; [13]cinnamon, spice, incense, myrrh, and frankincense; wine, olive oil, fine flour, and wheat; cattle and sheep, horses, and chariots, and slaves, that is, human beings.

[14]"The fruit you craved
    has left you.
All your luxury and splendor are gone,
    never again will one find them."

[15]The merchants who deal in these goods, who grew rich from her, will keep their distance for fear of the torment inflicted on her. Weeping and mourning, [16]they cry out:

"Alas, alas, great city,
    wearing fine linen, purple and scarlet,
    adorned [in] gold, precious stones,
    and pearls.
[17]In one hour this great wealth has been ruined."

Every captain of a ship, every traveler at sea, sailors, and seafaring merchants stood at a distance [18]and cried out when

for this whole sequence of laments is found in Ezek 26 and 27. The kings' lament alludes to Ezek 26:16. They see the city being destroyed by fire.

18:11-17a The merchants' lament. Like the kings of the earth, the merchants lament the overthrow of the great city. The description of her markets would suit any of the great trading ports of the Mediterranean. Her conquests in the East had made Rome famous as a center into which all the wealth and luxuries from those provinces flowed, even spices from faraway India. This great catalog of wares recalls that in Ezek 27. According to Ezek 27:13, Hellas demanded slaves.

Although no change of speaker is indicated, verse 14 appears out of place in the lament of the merchants. It probably represents an angelic condemnation like the longer one in verses 21-23.

Like the kings, the merchants draw back. They do not wish to share the fate of the city. They weep for all the great wealth that has been destroyed along with her.

18:17b-19 The seamen's lament. The final group to bewail the fate of the city are those whose ships bring her the wealth of the world. Each lament has followed the same pattern:

1. Introduction: "Alas, alas, great city . . ."
2. Statement of the relevant loss: kings—power; merchants—goods; shipowners—profit from trade.
3. Formal conclusion: "In one hour," destruction. The seamen's lament has a parallel in Ezek 27:29.

they saw the smoke of her pyre, "What city could compare with the great city?" ¹⁹They threw dust on their heads and cried out, weeping and mourning:

"Alas, alas, great city,
    in which all who had ships at sea grew rich from her wealth.
In one hour she has been ruined.
²⁰Rejoice over her, heaven,
    you holy ones, apostles, and prophets.
For God has judged your case against her."

²¹A mighty angel picked up a stone like a huge millstone and threw it into the sea and said:

"With such force will Babylon the great city be thrown down,
    and will never be found again.
²²No melodies of harpists and musicians, flutists and trumpeters,
    will ever be heard in you again.
No craftsmen in any trade
    will ever be found in you again.
No sound of the millstone
    will ever be heard in you again.

These laments paint a striking picture of the fall of a great trading center. Those who had benefited from her glory stand at a distance and watch her burn to the ground. Situated between two angelic proclamations of her judgment, they provide a strikingly human touch in the midst of an intense drama of divine and mythic symbols.

18:20-24 Rejoice! Babylon perishes! The call to rejoice contrasts with the laments of the previous section. It is the antitype of the rejoicing of the people in the city (= Jerusalem) over the death of the two witnesses in 11:8, and it contrasts with the call to rejoicing in 12:12. There the heavens could rejoice at the destruction of the beast, but those on earth had to expect woe. This call is the answer to the prayers of the saints. All who have suffered at the hands of the city are called to rejoice. The model for this summons appears in Deut 32:42; the nations are called to praise God for avenging the blood of her servants. Jer 51:48-49 summons the heavens and the earth to sing for joy over the destruction of Babylon. The legal grounds for the divine sentence, the "slain of Israel . . . the slain of all the earth" (Jer 51:49), is the same one that is found at the end of this passage. The city falls because of the blood of the prophets and saints.

The summons to rejoice and the legal sentence frame a final angelic cry as the destroying angel hurls a great millstone into the sea. The angel is enacting the conclusion to the great prophecy against Babylon in Jer 51:63-64. The prophet was told to bind the words of his prophecy against Babylon to a stone. As he cast the stone into the Euphrates, he was to say, "Thus shall Babylon sink. Never shall she rise, because of the evil I am bringing upon her." Rev 18:21 echoes those words, "With such force will Babylon the great city be thrown down, and will never be found again." The angel goes on to catalog the signs that she will never again rise as a city. That catalog continues to echo Ezek 27 with echoes from similar prophecies (see Isa 23:8,

²³No light from a lamp
  will ever be seen in you again.
No voices of bride and groom
  will ever be heard in you again.
Because your merchants were the great
  ones of the world,
  all nations were led astray by your
  magic potion.
²⁴In her was found the blood of prophets
  and holy ones
  and all who have been slain on the
  earth."

19 ¹After this I heard what sounded
like the voice of a great multitude
in heaven, saying:

  "Alleluia!
Salvation, glory, and might belong to
  our God,

² for true and just are his judgments.
He has condemned the great harlot
  who corrupted the earth with her
  harlotry.
He has avenged on her the blood of her
  servants."

³They said a second time:

"Alleluia! Smoke will rise from her forever and ever."

⁴The twenty-four elders and the four liv-
ing creatures fell down and worshiped
God who sat on the throne, saying,
"Amen. Alleluia."

The Victory Song. ⁵A voice coming
from the throne said:

"Praise our God, all you his servants,
  [and] you who revere him, small and
  great."

27; Jer 25:15-17; 49:38). This city will never rise from the ashes of its destruction.

Even the announced destruction of the great city does not bring the story
to its conclusion. The story of Revelation is about more than the fall of Roman
power. It is about the conflict between God and those faithful to him and
the forces of evil. The city embodies the beast, but the beast itself must be
destroyed. It is the activities of the beast which underlie all the empires that
are opposed to God. Before that story is told, we have another interlude
in heaven to give thanks for the divine act of salvation that has just been
described.

19:1-10 Hymn of divine victory. The heavenly assembly sings another
victory song. God's judgment and justice are praised. It is important to recognize the theological perspective of such a hymn. The avenging of the martyrs represents more than the personal desire to see a wrong punished. It
represents proof that God and his justice do rule the world. His judgments
of the glory and power of Rome are the right ones. Thus, such victory hymns
celebrate a world in which divine justice will win out in the affairs of humanity and nations, however much the evidence appears to go against that
truth.

Verse 4 returns us to the divine throne room. One of the creatures of
the throne calls to all the servants of God, all in the cosmos, to praise him
(see Ps 135:1). That call is answered with a psalm of rejoicing by the great
assembly (see Ps 118:24). Just as the earlier hymns had given us a glimpse

⁶Then I heard something like the sound of a great multitude or the sound of rushing water or might peals of thunder, as they said:

"Alleluia!
The Lord has established his reign, [our] God, the almighty.
⁷Let us rejoice and be glad
and give him glory.
For the wedding day of the Lamb has come,
his bride has made herself ready.
⁸She was allowed to wear
a bright, clean linen garment."

(The linen represents the righteous deeds of the holy ones.)
⁹Then the angel said to me, "Write this: Blessed are those who have been called to the wedding feast of the Lamb." And he said to me, "These words are true; they come from God." ¹⁰I fell at his feet to worship him. But he said to me, "Don't! I am a fellow servant of yours and of your brothers who bear witness to Jesus. Worship God. Witness to Jesus in the spirit of prophecy."

The King of Kings. ¹¹Then I saw the heavens opened, and there was a white

of the future victory of God, so this hymn gives us a glimpse of the salvation which is about to come, at the wedding feast of the Lamb. The bride is the antitype to the prostitute Babylon. That contrast will be made more explicit when the heavenly Jerusalem is revealed. Here the bride's dress is interpreted as the virtuous deeds of the righteous. They are to share in the salvation of the Lamb at that great wedding banquet. This scene also evokes another part of the ancient myth of the defeat of the monster of chaos, which is about to be played out. The victorious young god would celebrate a banquet on the divine mountain. Since fertility and new creation followed from the divine victory over the forces of chaos, some forms of the myth celebrate a sacred marriage as part of the manifestation of the new divine rule.

Verse 10 is somewhat awkward. Verse 9 would provide a suitable conclusion to the section with its beatitude on those who will partake of that feast. Suddenly the seer worships the angel. While such a response might occur at the first appearance of an angel to make a revelation, it hardly makes sense here. Certainly the seer knows that God and the Lamb are the objects of heavenly worship. Perhaps this verse represents an independent piece about the truth of Christian prophecy—every true spirit testifies to Jesus—that the author has included to authenticate his Christian vision of the victory of God over his enemies.

UNNUMBERED VISIONS

Rev 19:11–21:8

It indeed seems that "delay is the stuff of which Revelation is made." We find another series of visions before we see the bride at the wedding feast. These visions also reflect the mythic patterns of divine victory. God has yet to overthrow the monster and establish his divine presence on earth. The wedding feast can only take place as part of this final cycle, which brings the mythic allusions in the book to their completion. The mythic pattern of new creation also includes the building of a new temple to the god. Here the theme will be somewhat altered, since the new Jerusalem will be the dwelling place of the Lord. The basic elements of the pattern of divine combat and victory celebration can be found in the concluding sections of Revelation. They have been expanded by the addition of other materials, as is common in all the visions of Revelation. We actually have a double victory over the beast. Such a victory appears in some versions of the myth when the god must conquer chaos and death in separate battles. The basic elements in the pattern are:

1. Divine warrior appears (19:11-16)
2. Threat to divine sovereignty (19:19; 20:8-9a)
3. Combat and victory (19:20–20:3; 20:9b-10)
4. Victory shout (19:17-18)
5. Manifestation of divine kingship (20:4)
6. Salvation (20:5-6; 21:4; 22:1-5)
7. Renewal of creation/sacred marriage/building of temple (21:1-3, 9-27)

The victory shout actually comes before the divine victory rather than afterwards, as it would in the mythic stories. We have seen many examples of the "anticipation" of salvation, even the enthronement and kingship of the Lamb, in Revelation. Such anticipation forms part of the author's concern with assuring the audience of the present certainty of salvation.

When the author structures his story in accord with an archaic, mythic pattern as he has done here, we see that much more is involved than a simple prediction of historical events. The eternal realities imaged in that myth are shown to be fulfilled in the Christian story. The psychological power of those symbols to assure people of the order of the cosmos is evoked through the narrative. We no longer view the world in the dimensions of profane time or ordinary history. We view it from the perspective of divine time.

If the author is imaging Christian salvation as the fulillment of the most archaic, mythic hopes for salvation, then he has moved quite beyond the level of historical predictions. He has even moved beyond the level of social critique. The condemnation of Rome ended in chapter 18. Now, even the struggle with Rome is but an episode in the greater struggle with the primordial forces of evil and chaos for control of the world. Revelation was right about the Roman Empire, which had seemed both divine and immortal to many of its contemporaries. That empire, like all such empires, did collapse. Revelation is right: even the worst disasters will not turn those who do not

horse; its rider was [called] "Faithful and True." He judges and wages war in righteousness. ¹²His eyes were [like] a fiery flame, and on his head were many diadems. He had a name inscribed that no one knows except himself. ¹³He wore a cloak that had been dipped in blood, and his name was called the Word of God. ¹⁴The armies of heaven followed him, mounted on white horses and wearing clean white linen. ¹⁵Out of his mouth came a sharp sword to strike the nations. He will rule them with an iron rod, and he himself will tread out in the wine press the wine of the fury and wrath of God the almighty. ¹⁶He has a name written on his cloak and on his thigh, "King of kings and Lord of lords."

have prophetic insight into God's view of truth and justice to the Lord. Humanity can continue to ignore, or worse, to blaspheme God, even in the face of unspeakable horrors. When Revelation keeps asserting that the rule of God is victorious over evil, it does not do so out of a naïve optimism about humans and their behavior; rather, it claims that the only source of confidence in salvation can be the victory of God.

Now we come to the final movement in our journey, the final intensification of the images of salvation. Revelation shows us that all human hopes for salvation must be realized in the rule of God and the Lamb. The mythic patterns are taken up because, like the Old Testament prophecies, they are fulfilled in the Christian story of divine victory.

19:11-16 The messianic warrior. Christ wins the real victory in his death. Consequently, Revelation places much less emphasis on description of the messiah-warrior and his battle with the foes of the Lord than we might expect. Unlike other apocalypses of the period, the righteous do not participate in an earthly war paralleling the conflict of the divine warrior and Satan. All elements of conquest in this book are on the divine level. Human armies are not involved. This approach is quite different from the War Scroll that was found among the writings of the Essenes at the Dead Sea. That Jewish sect had a scroll which claimed to give instructions as to how the army of the righteous was to draw up for the wars that would be part of the messianic victory. It gave instructions about what was to be written on the trumpets and standards of the assembled hosts, and it included the hymns of victory that the army of the Lord would sing after defeating its enemies.

The Messiah finally appears for battle. Like the armies in the War Scroll, names are inscribed on his person and his equipment. But he comes only at the head of divine armies, not human ones. The names designate this rider as the source of divine salvation; he is not the earlier horseman of destruction (6:1-2). The description of the rider contains a string of his divine names: Faithful and True, Justice, unknown name, Word of God, and, finally, the divine acclamation, King of Kings, Lord of Lords. The unknown name may

¹⁷Then I saw an angel standing on the sun. He cried out [in] a loud voice to all the birds flying high overhead, "Come here. Gather for God's great feast, ¹⁸to eat the flesh of kings, the flesh of military officers, and the flesh of warriors, the flesh of horses and of their riders, and the flesh of all, free and slave, small and great." ¹⁹Then I saw the beast and the kings of the earth and their armies gathered to fight against the one riding the horse and against his army. ²⁰The beast was caught and with it the false prophet who had performed in its sight the signs by which he led astray those who had accepted the mark of the beast and those who had worshiped its image. The two were thrown alive into the fiery pool burning with sulfur. ²¹The rest were killed by the sword that came out of the mouth of the one riding the horse, and all the birds gorged themselves on their flesh.

20 **The Thousand-year Reign.** ¹Then I saw an angel come down from heaven, holding in his hand the key to the

refer to the "new name" God gives Jerusalem when he bestows salvation on her in Isa 62:2. All these names signify divine sovereignty and salvation.

The flaming eyes of Dan 10:6 are familiar from Rev 1:14 and 2:18. The messianic crown evokes the Psalms (Pss 21:4; 132:18), the title "King of Kings," and, of course, the many crowns worn by the beast. The rider goes forth to battle in blood-stained garments much as God does in Isa 63:1-3. The sword in the mouth recalls Isa 11:4 and 49:2; the rod, Ps 2:9. We are already familiar with the divine winepress from Rev 14:10 and 17:6 (see Isa 63:2; Joel 4:13). The combination of names, images and symbols attached to the divine warrior makes it clear that no one will escape this judgment. God is taking the field against the embodiment of evil.

19:17-21 The vultures' feast. As in the other mythic sections, this battle between the divine warrior and the beast is hardly described. Instead, ominous birds once more appear in midheaven. They are gathering to feast on the enemies of God (see Num 16:30; Isa 63:1-6). The curse against Gog in Ezek 39:4 warns that he will fall on the mountains of Israel and be given to the birds as food. So many will be killed that God will summon the birds and the wild beasts to come to a great sacrificial feast, to dine on the bodies of the fallen warriors and their horses (Ezek 39:17-20). So here the birds are summoned to feast on all who had followed the beast. Some interpreters suggest that this feast is a gruesome parody of the heavenly victory feast that follows the defeat of the beast in the mythic cycle. Once again, a delay; the inhuman enemies of the divine warrior, the beast, and the false prophet are not slain but imprisoned in Hades.

20:1-6 A thousand-year reign. This section has combined several apocalyptic themes. Speculation about a thousand-year reign of the Messiah is uncommon. However, the section of Ezekiel on which the author has been drawing does contain a doubling of the end-time images of salvation:

abyss and a heavy chain. ²He seized the dragon, the ancient serpent, which is the Devil or Satan, and tied it up for a thousand years ³and threw it into the abyss, which he locked over it and sealed, so that it could no longer lead the nations astray until the thousand years are completed. After this, it is to be released for a short time.

⁴Then I saw thrones; those who sat on them were entrusted with judgment. I also saw the souls of those who had been beheaded for their witness to Jesus and for the word of God, and who had not worshiped the beast or its image nor had ac-

cepted its mark on their foreheads or hands. They came to life and they reigned with Christ for a thousand years. ⁵The rest of the dead did not come to life until the thousand years were over. This is the first resurrection. ⁶Blessed and holy is the one who shares in the first resurrection. The second death has no power over these; they will be priests of God and of Christ, and they will reign with him for [the] thousand years.

⁷When the thousand years are completed, Satan will be released from his prison. ⁸He will go out to deceive the nations at the four corners of the earth, Gog

the Messiah rules; Gog and Magog are defeated; the new Jerusalem is described (Ezek 37–43). This passage in Revelation pictures a rule by the Messiah prior to the defeat of Gog and Magog. Before that reign can occur, an angel imprisons the dragon in the abyss. He resembles the star-like angel with the keys to the abyss in Rev 9:1. The descent into Hades continues the imagery of Satan's fall from 12:9.

The significance of the throne imagery in this passage is not clear. At the end of the last letter, the victors are promised that they will share the throne of God/Jesus (3:21). Traditionally, the righteous or some group of them ascended thrones to judge the wicked (see Dan 7:9, the beast; Matt 19:28-30, the nations; also 1 Cor 6:2). Though Revelation has those sitting on thrones empowered to pass judgment, it is not clear whom they would be judging, since the messianic kingdom is established on earth, and the final judgment is yet to be described.

This section also seems to have mixed traditions about the resurrection. Images of resurrection in the first century vary between a general resurrection for a judgment, which separates righteous from wicked people, and resurrection as the reward for the righteous. The awkward distinctions in verses 4 and 5 may represent a combination of both traditions. The faithful witnesses are rewarded with an early resurrection and share the thousand-year reign. Verse 6 makes it clear that that resurrection is a definitive sign of salvation. Others will be resurrected at the judgment.

20:7-10 Against Gog and Magog. As in the previous battle scene, there is little description of the actual battle. In the tradition upon which Revelation draws (Ezek 38:22, 39), the armies are made up of people from among the nations. Either Revelation assumes that some have survived the previous destruction, since the dragon is said to be prevented from leading the

and Magog, to gather them for battle; their number is like the sand of the sea. ⁹They invaded the breadth of the earth and surrounded the camp of the holy ones and the beloved city. But fire came down from heaven and consumed them. ¹⁰The Devil who had led them astray was thrown into the pool of fire and sulfur, where the beast and the false prophet were. There they will be tormented day and night forever and ever.

The Large White Throne. ¹¹Next I saw a large white throne and the one who was sitting on it. The earth and the sky fled from his presence and there was no place for them. ¹²I saw the dead, the great and the lowly, standing before the throne, and scrolls were opened. Then another scroll was opened, the book of life. The dead were judged according to their deeds, by what was written in the scrolls. ¹³The sea gave up its dead; then Death and Hades gave up their dead. All the dead were judged according to their deeds. ¹⁴Then Death and Hades were thrown into the pool of fire. (This pool of fire is the second death.) ¹⁵Anyone whose name was not found written in the book of life was thrown into the pool of fire.

VI: THE NEW CREATION

21 The New Heaven and the New Earth.

¹Then I saw a new heaven and a new earth. The former heaven and the former earth had passed away, and the sea was no more. ²I also saw the holy city, a new Jerusalem, coming down out of heaven from God, prepared as a bride adorned for her husband. ³I heard a loud

nations astray, or one must assume that this army is made up of the dead/resurrected. The traditional image has the nations draw up against the people of God who are with the Messiah in Jerusalem (= the beloved city). That seems to be the tradition behind this battle. Revelation does not specify the nature of the opposition any further. What is significant is the final and eternal imprisonment of the devil, the beast, and the false prophet.

20:11-15 Judgment of the dead. God appears on his throne to execute judgment (compare Dan 7:9). This image of judgment presupposes a universal judgment of all those who are dead, wherever they may be. All that is hostile to God is cast into the fire of judgment, the second—and real—death. This punishment includes the destruction of both death as enemy and the underworld (see Isa 25:8; 1 Cor 15:26).

21:1-5a New heaven and earth. This section closes with the vision of a new heaven and earth that replaces the old creation, which has finally passed away (see Isa 65:17). The author is not interested in the implications of the image of a new creation which he has taken from Isaiah. Consequently, we cannot push this verse for information about the renewal of the natural world, as some interpreters concerned with ecology have tried to do. The real center-piece of the new creation is the new Jerusalem (see Isa 52:1-3). The holy city will be the true dwelling place of God and also of the bride in the final section of the work. The throne voice announces that the promises of divine presence are fulfilled in this city (see Ezek 37:27; Zech 2:14; Jer 38:33). This voice from the throne saying, "Behold, God's dwelling is with the human race. He will dwell with them and they will be his people and God himself will always be with them [as their God]. ⁴He will wipe every tear from their eyes, and there shall be no more death or mourning, wailing or pain, [for] the old order has passed away."

⁵The one who sat on the throne said, "Behold, I make all things new." Then he said, "Write these words down, for they are trustworthy and true." ⁶He said to me, "They are accomplished. I [am] the Al-pha and the Omega, the beginning and the end. To the thirsty I will give a gift from the spring of life-giving water. ⁷The victor will inherit these gifts, and I shall be his God, and he will be my son. ⁸But as for cowards, the unfaithful, the depraved, murderers, the unchaste, sorcerers, idol-worshipers, and deceivers of every sort, their lot is in the burning pool of fire and sulfur, which is the second death."

The New Jerusalem. ⁹One of the seven angels who held the seven bowls filled with the seven last plagues came and said

city of divine presence and peace forms a striking contrast to the fallen Babylon (see Isa 25:8; 35:10; 65:19). In Isa 43:18-19 the Lord tells Israel not to remember the old things, since he is doing "a new thing." Revelation proclaims that that promise is finally fulfilled. God is making all things new.

21:5b-8 Second conclusion. These last chapters anticipate the conclusion of the whole with injunctions to the seer to record the trustworthy vision which he has received (see 19:9). The following section resumes the vision of the bride of the Lamb with an introduction that is parallel to the vision of the whore of Babylon (compare 21:9 and 17:1). This interruption also provides Revelation the opportunity to anticipate the bridal scene and the marriage feast (already anticipated once in the hymn of 19:7-8). The command to write and the divine name Alpha and Omega also bring us back to the beginning of the book (1:11, 19). The exhortations in this section are reminders of the exhortations in the opening letters, as are the promises to the victors (largely derived from the prophetic sayings in Isa 55:1-6). The passage seems to recapitulate the warnings of those letters. Verse 8 warns against various vices and idolatry. Thus, the section reminds the audience that the lessons of the book are to be applied to their own situation. They must heed the revelation and repent, lest they find themselves excluded from the final salvation. Now we find one final image of that final salvation, the new Jerusalem.

THE NEW JERUSALEM

Rev 21:9–22:5

We finally see the new Jerusalem in all her glory. This vision of the city in which God truly dwells rounds out the condemnation of all the false claims

to me, "Come here. I will show you the bride, the wife of the Lamb." [10]He took me in spirit to a great, high mountain and showed me the holy city Jerusalem coming down out of heaven from God. [11]It gleamed with the splendor of God. Its radiance was like that of a precious stone, like jasper, clear as crystal. [12]It had a massive, high wall, with twelve gates where twelve angels were stationed and on which names were inscribed, [the names] of the twelve tribes of the Israelites. [13]There were three gates facing east, three north, three south, and three west. [14]The wall of the city had twelve courses of stones as its foundation, on which were inscribed the twelve names of the twelve apostles of the Lamb.

[15]The one who spoke to me held a gold measuring rod to measure the city, its gates, and its wall. [16]The city was square, its length the same as [also] its width. He measured the city with the rod and found it fifteen hundred miles in length and width and height. [17]He also measured its wall: one hundred and forty-four cubits according to the standard unit of measurement the angel used. [18]The wall was constructed of jasper, while the city was pure gold, clear as glass. [19]The foundations of the city wall were decorated with every precious stone; the first course of stones was jasper, the second sapphire, the third chalcedony, the fourth emerald, [20]the fifth sardonyx, the sixth carnelian, the seventh chrysolite, the eighth beryl, the ninth topaz, the tenth chrysoprase, the eleventh hyacinth, and the twelfth amethyst. [21]The twelve gates were twelve pearls, each of the gates made from a single pearl; and the street of the city was of pure gold, transparent as glass.

[22]I saw no temple in the city, for its temple is the Lord God almighty and the Lamb. [23]The city had no need of sun or moon to shine on it, for the glory of God

of the beast and Babylon in the previous chapters. It also represents the final gathering of the community which belongs to the Lamb.

21:9-21 The bride of the Lamb. The introduction to the vision of the bride deliberately recalls the introduction to the vision of the whore of Babylon. The two cities are antitypes of one another. Much of the imagery of the city also derives from Ezekiel: the city on the mount from 40:2; the city full of the glory of God from 43:2-4. The description of the walls primarily draws upon Ezek 40:5; 48:31-35, though other prophetic descriptions of the walls of Jerusalem might also lie behind this passage (see Jer 30:18; Isa 26:1; 60:10, 18; 62:6). Angelic watchers appear in Ezek 49:12 (also Isa 62:6, 10). Ezekiel's gates represent the twelve tribes (43:31-34). For Revelation, the Twelve are the apostles. The use of Ezekiel imagery has switched from description of the woman as bride to the architectural features that define the city.

The next actions continue that image. Like Ezekiel (ch. 40), the seer measures the city. The measurements emphasize the perfection and size of the city. The stones in the walls seem to be based on Exod 28:17-20 (also 39:10-13; 36:17-20). Some interpreters try to give astrological interpretations of the various stones. If the author was acquainted with such traditions, he does not give any indication that he is exploiting that symbolism in the description about the city.

gave it light, and its lamp was the Lamb. [24]The nations will walk by its light, and to it the kings of the earth will bring their treasure. [25]During the day its gates will never be shut, and there will be no night there. [26]The treasure and wealth of the nations will be brought there, [27]but nothing unclean will enter it, nor any[one] who does abominable things or tells lies. Only those will enter whose names are written in the Lamb's book of life.

22 [1]Then the angel showed me the river of life-giving water, sparkling like crystal, flowing from the throne of God and of the Lamb [2]down the middle of its street. On either side of the river grew the tree of life that produces fruit twelve times a year, once each month; the leaves of the trees serve as medicine for the nations. [3]Nothing accursed will be found there anymore. The throne of God and of the Lamb will be in it, and his servants will worship him. [4]They will look upon his face, and his name will be on their foreheads. [5]Night will be no more, no will they need light from lamp or sun, for the Lord God shall give them light, and they shall reign forever and ever.

21:22-27 Divine presence in the city. This city is introduced as quite different from its prototype in Ezekiel when we learn that there is no temple there. The presence of God and of the Lamb makes the whole city a temple. Metaphors derived from Isaiah are used to describe the divine presence in the city; the basic passage is 60:1-20. Most of the elements of this passage can be found there. The glory of the Lord fills Jerusalem, so that she has no need of heavenly bodies to provide light (60:19-20; also Isa 24:33). The kings of the earth come bringing their wealth (60:3, 11). The city gates are always open (60:11a). The city is one of holiness. Nothing profane enters. Only the righteous live in this city (60:21; also Isa 35:8; 52:1; Ezek 44:9). Revelation has taken the vision of Isaiah and made appropriate additions to suit the images of the Lamb and the book of life. In so doing, it has proclaimed that vision fulfilled. The glory of divine presence is shared between God and the Lamb. The righteous who dwell in the city are faithful Christians.

22:1-5 The water and the trees of life. The vision of the new Jerusalem concludes with an image of the blessedness and immortality of those who inhabit it. The life-giving water flowing from the thrones of God and the Lamb recall the image of the streams of water flowing from the temple mount in Joel 4:18 and Ezek 47 (also Jer 2:13; Pss 46:5; 36:10). The tree of life from Gen 2:9 has been combined with the trees by the stream from Ezek 47:12 to provide twelve fruit-bearing trees. They provide the healing predicted for the pagan nations in Joel 1:14; 2:15. Just as nothing profane can enter the city, so nothing cursed can dwell in the grove near the stream (see Zech 14:11). These final verses bring Revelation to a fitting close by summarizing the promises that have been made to the elect throughout the work. Those promises are all fulfilled in the heavenly city.

VII: EPILOGUE

⁶And he said to me, "These words are trustworthy and true, and the Lord, the God of prophetic spirits, sent his angel to show his servants what must happen soon." ⁷"Behold, I am coming soon." Blessed is the one who keeps the prophetic message of this book.

⁸It is I, John, who heard and saw these things, and when I heard and saw them I fell down to worship at the feet of the angel who showed them to me. ⁹But he said to me, "Don't! I am a fellow servant of yours and of your brothers the prophets and of those who keep the message of this book. Worship God."

¹⁰Then he said to me, "Do not seal up the prophetic words of this book, for the appointed time is near. ¹¹Let the wicked still act wickedly, and the filthy still be filthy. The righteous must still do right, and the holy still be holy."

¹²Behold, I am coming soon. I bring with me the recompense I will give to each according to his deeds. ¹³I am the Alpha and the Omega, the first and the last, the beginning and the end."

EPILOGUE

Rev 22:6-21

Revelation concludes with a collection of separate prophetic oracles. They testify to the authenticity of the revelation contained in the book. The speaker shifts from oracle to oracle. We hear words of the revealing angel, of Jesus, of the Spirit, and of the prophet. Three themes are reiterated throughout: heed the revelation; the end is near; the righteous are rewarded. The "I am coming soon" of the opening exhortations ties this conclusion back to the initial revelation (1:1; 2:16; 3:11; 22:6b, 7, 12, 20).

The nearness of the Lord's coming is often tied to exhortations to remain faithful. That combination suggests that the phrase was part of the regular ethical exhortation of the churches addressed. It was not primarily directed at calculating exactly when the end would be; rather, the phrase assures the audience of the Lord's coming so that they will continue to be faithful. In Rev 2:16 it belongs to the exhortation against the Nicolaitan heresy. In Rev 3:11 it encourages perseverance.

As in the conclusion to Daniel (12:5), the author signs his name to the revelation to attest to its authenticity. Unlike Daniel (12:10), the words of the revelation are not sealed. For the second time the seer is rebuked for worshiping the revealing angel (also 19:10). Both the angels and the faithful stand together in praising God, as we have seen throughout the book in the scenes of the heavenly liturgy.

The oracle confirming the division between righteous and wicked in the last days also confirms a phenomenon to which the visions have given us dramatic testimony. The various plagues did not bring humanity to repen-

Beatitude ¹⁴Blessed are they who wash their robes so as to have the right to the tree of life and enter the city through its gates. ¹⁵Outside are the dogs, the sorcerers, the unchaste, the murderers, the idol-worshipers, and all who love and practice deceit.

¹⁶"I, Jesus, sent my angel to give you this testimony for the churches. I am the root and offspring of David, the bright morning star."

¹⁷The Spirit and the bride say, "Come." Let the hearer say, "Come." Let the one who thirsts come forward and the one who wants it receive the gift of life-giving water.

¹⁸I warn everyone who hears the prophetic words in this book: if anyone adds

tance. The prophecy does not convert the wicked from their ways (compare Ezek 3:27; Dan 12:10).

Jesus speaks with his divine authority, Alpha and Omega, to affirm the reward that is to be given to each. The beatitude (v. 14) is a variant of 7:14, which now includes the new visions of the holy city, in which nothing profane dwells with the tree of life. Verse 15 cites a catalog of vices to indicate the evils that cannot be allowed to enter the new city (cf. Joel 3:22–4:17; Rev 21:7-8).

Verse 16 has Jesus authenticate the angel of 1:1 as his messenger. The messianic titles given Jesus come from the Old Testament: root of Jesse (Isa 11:10); star of Jacob (Num 24:17); morning star (Isa 9:1; 60:1).

The summons to "come" in verse 17 allude to the liturgical practice of summoning the righteous to the Eucharist. Here we find an antiphonal summons to come and receive the promised reward. Another part of the same liturgy was the prayer to the Lord to come. Paul indicates that it was spoken in Aramaic, *Marana tha*, "Lord, come!" (1 Cor 16:22). It was also connected with the pronouncement of a formula excluding all nonbelievers and all who are not holy. The catalog of vices in verse 15 could function as such a formula for Revelation. Thus, the audience is reminded that the summons into the liturgical assembly is an image of that final summons to the gathering of the holy ones of God. We are also reminded that Revelation was read in such a community gathering.

The final verses provide further testimony to the truth of the prophecy. The curse against those who tamper with the words of such a revelation derives from Deut 4:2. Such curses also appear in Jewish apocryphal writings from New Testament times. Jesus' own testimony to the truth of the revelation is answered by the liturgical prayer for his coming. A common conclusion in Pauline letters ends Revelation. It reminds us, as much of the epilogue has, that the revelation is given to the audience which has also heard the warnings and promises in the letters. They must apply these visions to their situation. Those who are praised should continue, confident in the salvation that they have been promised. Those who are called to repent should heed

to them, God will add to him the plagues described in this book, [19]and if anyone takes away from the words in this prophetic book, God will take away his share in the tree of life and in the holy city described in this book.

[20]The one who gives this testimony says, "Yes, I am coming soon." Amen! Come, Lord Jesus!

[21]The grace of the Lord Jesus be with all.

the warning, lest they be found among the hardened and blasphemous who will not listen to any of the words of the Lord.

The message of Revelation does not depend upon calculations about the time of the second coming of the Lord. People must be convinced about the "nearness of the Lord" and the certainty of the Christian vision of salvation if they are to heed the warnings in the book. Many of the questions raised by Revelation continue to create problems for Christians. They must question false claims of political and economic systems when they destroy values that Christians are committed to. They must question the nature of human compliance with evil and injustice. Christians must also face the dangers of sectarian groups which pervert the gospel by claiming to have esoteric wisdom not available to others, "to know the depths of God." They must also ask whether they really believe in God's rule over the cosmos, which Revelation presents as real and active. Or, perhaps, Christians really feel that God is "far off" and not really concerned with the problems of our day beyond some record-keeping of individual transgressions. Perhaps the justice demanded in the prophets to whom Revelation is constantly alluding does not seem to count for much in the complexities of the modern world. Revelation would never tolerate such an attitude among Christians. It has used all the mythic and symbolic resources at its disposal to show Christians the dangers of a false estimate of the powers of this world. Christians live on the edge of times. They take their values from the gospel and from the way God sees things. They should always expect that "the Lord is coming soon!"

REVIEW AIDS AND DISCUSSION TOPICS

I

Introduction (pages 5–12)

1. How does Revelation resemble a movie? Give two examples.
2. What is an apocalypse? Name the apocalypse that is in the Old Testament.
3. How do apocalypses understand martyrdom? The Roman Empire?
4. Who was the emperor when Revelation was written? What was his rule like?
5. What was emperor worship? Why did it create problems for Christians?

II

1:1-8 Prologue (pages 13–16)

1. What are the two parts of the prologue?
2. What does "revelation" mean?
3. What is the significance of the theme testimony or witness in Revelation?
4. To whom is Revelation addressed?
5. What is the message about God and salvation presented in the prologue?

III

1:9-3:22 The Letters to the Churches (pages 16–26)

1. What does the call vision tell us about the author of Revelation?
2. Compare the opening description of Jesus with Dan 7:9-14 and 10:5-6. What does the description of Jesus in Revelation tell us about him?
3. Pick out three examples of the contrast life/death in the letters. What are Christians to learn from that contrast?
4. Describe two different problems facing the church in Asia Minor.
5. How would you apply the teaching of the letters to Christians today?

IV

4:1-8:5 The Seven Seals (pages 26–41)

1. How do apocalypses use cycles of visions? How do such cycles relate to historical events?
2. Study the visions of the throne and the Lamb. What Jewish traditions has Revelation used in these visions?
3. List all the examples of heavenly praise found in this section. What is the message of each hymn of praise? How is that message related to the vision which comes before it?
4. Describe the concrete, human experiences reflected in the vision of the four horsemen.

5. What is the reader to learn from the visions of the "martyrs under the altar" and the "144,000"?

6. Why does the content of the seventh seal come as a surprise?

V

8:6–11:19 The Seven Trumpets (*pages* 41–49)

1. What is the basis for the plagues in this section? What do we learn from the plague visions?

2. How does Revelation move into the realm of mythological symbols? Give two examples.

3. What do the symbols used in the commissioning of the prophet tell us? How do apocalypses use the symbolic time period of three and a half years?

4. Describe the sign of the two witnesses. Why does that vision inspire terror?

5. What is the message of the hymn to the Lamb?

VI

12:1–15:4 Unnumbered Visions (*pages* 49–63)

1. What mythological stories would the audience have associated with the "woman clothed with the sun"? What is the message conveyed by that symbol?

2. What is the meaning of the dragon/beast from the sea in Jewish apocalypses?

3. What do we learn about the dragon from the heavenly victory in 12:7-12?

4. How is the Nero legend symbolized in the beast? Give three examples.

5. What message does the image of the beast carry regarding the emperor cult? Why might Christians have been tempted to engage in venerating the emperor?

6. What promise does Revelation hold out for those who resist worshiping the beast?

VII

15:5–16:21 The Seven Bowls (*pages* 63–67)

1. What is the message of the bowl plagues? How do they compare with plague visions earlier in Revelation?

2. What is the symbolism behind the plague of the armies in the East (16:12-16)?

3. How do the sixth and seventh plagues prepare the reader for what is to come?

VIII

17:1–19:10 Babylon the Great (*pages* 67–74)

1. Describe the Old Testament images used in the picture of Babylon.

2. How do we know that Babylon stands for Rome? What is the significance of the heads of the beast?

3. What are the reasons given for the destruction of the great city? What is the relationship between those who mourn her destruction and the city?

4. What is the message of the victory hymn which concludes this section?

5. Why does Revelation continue on after the destruction of Babylon?

IX

19:11–21:8 Unnumbered Visions (pages 74–80)

1. What mythic pattern lies behind this section? Why does the author use that pattern?

2. How is Christ's messianic victory different from the victories of the mythic heroes?

3. What is the relationship between resurrection and judgment in this section of Revelation?

4. How does the final vision of judgment remind the reader of the letters at the beginning of Revelation?

X

21:9–22:5 The New Jerusalem (pages 80–82)

1. Why is the new Jerusalem vision an appropriate ending to Revelation?

2. What is new about God's presence with his people in this vision?

3. How are the earlier promises of salvation fulfilled in this vision? Give two examples.

XI

22:6-21 Epilogue (pages 83–85)

1. How does the epilogue bring the audience back from the heavenly vision to the realities of daily Christian life?

2. What is the liturgical background of the prayer "Lord, come!"?

3. How would you describe the message of Revelation for Christians today?

(end of September)

The Feast of the TABERNACLES: (Boothes)

⇒ remind of the yrs. in desert
⇒ historical = 40yrs. of wondering (between God
                                    and His people)
— this must be a sign of when the Messiah
               comes

— confession of Messiahship = waving of palm
                                          branches
                                          (Palm
                                           Sunday)

Rev. 7:9 = palm branches...⇒ symbol of
                                      victory

Rev. 4: 6b -8   = ① Taurus
(Page 33)   ② Leo
                   ③ Scorpio
                   ④ Eagle

FAST & FURIOUS
SPY RACERS

TESTED

by Landry Q. Walker
Illustrated by
Patrick Spaziante

PENGUIN YOUNG READERS LICENSES
An Imprint of Penguin Random House LLC, New York

Penguin supports copyright. Copyright fuels creativity, encourages diverse voices, promotes free speech, and creates a vibrant culture. Thank you for buying an authorized edition of this book and for complying with copyright laws by not reproducing, scanning, or distributing any part of it in any form without permission. You are supporting writers and allowing Penguin to continue to publish books for every reader.

The publisher does not have any control over and does not assume any responsibility for author or third-party websites or their content.

Photo credit: cover (texture on title) OlgaSalt/iStock/Getty Images Plus

Fast & Furious franchise © 2020 Universal City Studios LLC.
TV Series © 2020 DreamWorks Animation LLC. All Rights Reserved.

Published by Penguin Young Readers Licenses, an imprint of
Penguin Random House LLC, New York. Manufactured in China.

Visit us online at www.penguinrandomhouse.com.

ISBN 9780593222508   10 9 8 7 6 5 4 3 2 1

CHAPTER 1

Cisco almost dropped his Froyo as he looked up at the enormous and intimidating machine. "You guys are climbing into that thing? For real?"

"Cisco has a point," Frostee added. "This machine is pretty teched-out and all, but the force from being spun that fast in a circle?"

"Right?" Cisco agreed. "You'll be so dizzy, you'll be turned inside out!"

Tony appraised the giant machine and the pod that was attached to it. He couldn't help agreeing with his friends—it didn't exactly look like it would be fun. The rocket-shaped pod was bolted to an arm that was attached to an enormous centrifuge—a machine designed to spin and spin.

A machine that he was supposed to sit inside.

Basically, it was a machine designed to

make you want to hurl your guts out.

"Come on!" Echo Pearl teased. "We've driven off of cliffs. This is totally safe! We'll be fine!" She glanced at the machine. "But you go first."

Ms. Nowhere was looming behind the pair, though she was mostly typing away in some private conversation. Still, she managed to respond with her usual charm. "It's a two-seater," she said. "And you're both getting in it. Together."

Echo's wide smile faded. "Then I find this situation entirely less amusing," the young artist answered.

Tony continued to glance suspiciously at the exceedingly dangerous-looking pod. "We've totally proven ourselves over and over again, right? We've never really failed a mission . . ."

Ms. Nowhere scoffed. "What about that one in San Diego? During Comic-Con? All you had to do was monitor the sale of that experimental fuel filter. Instead . . ."

Tony managed to look hurt. "Totally not

our fault!" he argued. "There were other factors!"

Echo nodded. "There was no way we could know that the submarine was controlled by robots."

"Or that the warehouse was going to be filled with rare movie props," Tony agreed.

"Why would you even put the smuggler ship from *Outspaced 4* in a warehouse?" Frostee added, a rising tone of incredulity in his voice. "It belongs in a museum!"

Cisco raised an eyebrow. "I don't know, man. *Outspaced 4* was not the best in the franchise. Too much of a political agenda."

Layla, who had been otherwise quiet, suddenly looked at her friend. "Oh, don't you start with me, Cisco!" She glared at him. "That movie redefined pop culture!"

"Enough!" Ms. Nowhere roared, stepping between the two teenagers. "It's not up to you to judge the merits of the test. It's up to you to take it!"

"*They* don't have to take it," Tony objected, pointing at Frostee, Cisco, and Layla.

Nowhere rolled her eyes. "Their skills have been tested in a dozen different ways. You're all under examination all the time. That's the way this stuff works when you're a teenager working under adult supervision, okay?"

Both Echo and Tony shifted uncomfortably.

"Your confidence is so incredibly reassuring," Ms. Nowhere said, clearly exasperated. "Cisco, Frostee, Layla, please exit. You can watch the test from the safety of the observation deck."

Before any of them could object, she raised her hand and waved them away.

"Okay," Layla said, giving Tony's shoulder a quick squeeze and throwing a reassuring look at Echo. "You both are going to do great. I'm sure of it."

Frostee shook his head. "I'm *way* less sure of it. But whatever. Hey, Cisco, let's go get some waffles!"

As the three teenagers exited the testing chambers, a stranger walked into the room—a tall man with a white lab coat and thick-framed glasses. "Meet Dr. David Rowan," Ms. Nowhere said. "David is the head engineer and software designer for this testing facility, and he will be monitoring your results."

"Hello, young people," Dr. Rowan said. "Are you ready to begin? My machine will test your limits in ways you cannot even imagine. It'll be fun."

Tony shrugged. "Well, it's totally safe no matter what, right? I mean, we drive cars in the real world. I think we can handle it. It's basically like a theme park ride."

"Perhaps. The controls are fairly self-explanatory," the engineer said with a thin smile. "For a driver of your caliber, I'm sure it should be simple."

"*Pff!*" Tony replied. "Totally, I'm sure."

With that, Ms. Nowhere and Dr. Rowan walked out of the room, and Echo and Tony were left to climb into the strange pod. Inside was a steel cage for reinforcement, and two heavy-looking leather seats with padded harnesses in place. The console was made up of a variety of levers, buttons, and switches. More notably, there were two steering wheels.

The pair strapped themselves in. A moment later, the pod automatically closed itself. In the distance, Tony and Echo both could hear a faint humming, the sound of a very large and very powerful engine warming up.

The voice of David Rowan boomed through the pod's speaker system. *"Everything is ready. The test will begin in ten seconds. I suggest you try to relax. It might get . . . uncomfortable."*

Echo tensed. Tony looked over at her and smiled warmly. He put his hands on the steering wheel. "Don't worry," he said. "We got this thing under—"

But before he could finish his sentence, the massive engine engaged, and the pod began to spin. Two point three seconds later, the pod was whizzing around and around the gigantic room at over four hundred miles per hour, and Tony and Echo began to black out.

CHAPTER 2

Tony felt himself beginning to black out. The pod was spinning impossibly fast. He tried to grab his steering wheel, but it yanked out of his grasp. He glanced over. "Echo?" he managed through gritted teeth. "You okay? I think you gotta turn your wheel when I turn mine."

"*Blurg,*" Echo managed to say. "*Guh,*" she added, for clarity's sake.

"Okay," Tony said as the pod whipped around the massive centrifuge. "We're supposed to do what with this now?"

The light on the dashboard in front of Tony conveniently blinked blue.

"Okay," Tony muttered. "Okay, so I press this and . . ."

Tony pressed the button and immediately wished that he hadn't. The entire pod rotated upside down. Then it began to bounce.

"Dr. Rowan, this is not fun!" Tony heard himself shout.

"Just part of the test," Rowan said through the intercom, with a low chuckle. *"All you have to do is try to maintain your concentration. Focus."*

"Please . . . shut it down," Echo mumbled.

"No!" Tony called as a surge of adrenaline shot through him. "We can do this. Echo, you with me?"

Echo managed a slight shake of her head. "Nope," she said quietly. "Too much spinning."

Tony looked at the control panel. Every light was blinking. Everything was spinning. He felt beyond dizzy.

"So we have to pilot . . . drive . . . steer this stupid pod. And it's a two-person control system." Tony eyed the steering wheels. There was no way he could operate both at the same time. That was the trick! *That* was why the test was so difficult. It took two people operating in perfect synchronicity. "So improvise," Tony managed to say to himself.

With a quick twist, Tony yanked at his belt buckle. The leather belt came free under the heavy seat straps easily enough. Reaching over, Tony looped Echo's steering wheel, twisting it in the process. Then he threaded the belt through a gap in his own steering wheel.

With a deft twist of his wrist, he pulled the belt tight and spun his wheel. Echo's wheel spun in sync. Suddenly, the pod started to stabilize.

Echo struggled to speak. "What?" she mumbled. "You got it?"

"Not quite yet!" Tony shouted.

He noticed the buttons on both consoles were flashing in sequence. The sequence was the same on both consoles.

"Echo!" he yelled. "You need to hit the buttons."

"Okay," she said, still struggling. "Pressing red."

"Now blue," Tony yelled.

"And yellow," Echo added.

"What are you doing?" David Rowan yelled

through the intercom. *"You aren't supposed to be able to do that!"*

"Green!" Tony and Echo both yelled, slamming the last button in the sequence at the same time.

A loud horn sounded in the distance, and the pod slowed to a halt. It opened with a hiss, and the security harness straps automatically released.

Dr. Rowan stormed down the stairs, sweat on his forehead.

"Cheaters!" the engineer yelled. "You cheated! There is no way you could have overcome the disabling effects. My machine is better than any driver!"

Ms. Nowhere followed closely behind. "Rowan! This is completely inappropriate!"

"But they had to have cheated!"

"I'm as surprised as you," Nowhere interjected dryly. "But the test is a challenge of endurance and innovation. *How* they pass isn't an issue."

Dr. Rowan frowned. Tony and Echo were both out of the pod now, though neither was feeling particularly steady on their feet.

"But—" Rowan started.

"No," Ms. Nowhere mused. "I found this very illuminating. David, put together a full report of the process they used to shut the machine down."

The engineer threw one last look of anger at Tony, then stormed off.

"So, did we pass?" Tony asked Ms. Nowhere. "I mean, we did it! We took control of the thing and we passed, right?"

Ms. Nowhere tapped her foot. "I'm not unimpressed with your performance, Tony. Head to the debriefing chambers and we will discuss your results."

"Awesome!" Tony said, smiling. "You hear that, Echo? We did great! Come on, let's go chill."

Tony headed for the door, with a wide smile on his face, but Ms. Nowhere reached out and placed a hand on Echo's shoulder, stopping the young girl from following her friend.

"One moment, Echo," Ms. Nowhere started to say.

"You don't need to say it," Echo murmured. "I know . . . I wasn't good enough."

And with that, Echo followed Tony out the door.

CHAPTER 3

"You see that?" a voice whispered. "They both responded so differently. Is that—"

"It's within the predictive norms. The test's reactions are always different, based on the individual. But the metrics of the results remain consistent."

"You're certain? This needs to be a fair assessment or it's meaningless."

"One hundred percent. If the reaction was identical, that would be a much larger concern. The nature of this . . ." The man speaking took a moment and adjusted a dial on a large computer console. In response, a series of lights fluctuated. Satisfied, he continued. "The point is, the story that unfolds for each subject is driven by the subconscious of the individual. Just wait, you'll see."

"And they are completely locked in their hypnotic states?"

"That's what the pod really does. They think they've already completed the test, but they'll keep spinning for as long as we need them to. They will see and feel everything as if they were somewhere else. And we can monitor *that* reaction."

Ms. Nowhere nodded. "Okay, then, Dr. Rowan. Let's continue."

CHAPTER 4

Tony felt on top of the world. He had aced the test, apparently breaking all the records of endurance as he did so. Then he had gorged himself at the ice-cream bar, spent a couple of hours playing video games, and even read the newest issue of his favorite comic book, *Gamma Blast Three*. It was a pretty great day.

And then the power went out.

Which was a weird thing to happen in the lair of a government shadow operation.

Tony poked his head out of the rec room. It was quiet. Where had everyone gone? He tapped his spy watch. "Hey, Layla? Echo?" Nothing. Just static. "Ms. Nowhere?" he tried. Still nothing.

And then the static broke, and a deep voice hissed at him through his spy watch. *"No one is here to help you, Tony. No way for you to cheat, either."*

Tony blinked. "Rowan? Dr. Rowan, right?" The lights flickered. The hallway of the facility was empty. "Hey, Dr. Rowan. What's going on?"

At the end of the hallway, a monitor switched on, and it broadcast the very angry face of Dr. Rowan.

"That test was my life's work. It was everything to me. I built a machine that was unbeatable."

"I mean, you really didn't," Tony replied.

"You cheated! The test was supposed to be defeated by two people, working in tandem, as a team. You bypassed that with your little belt trick!"

The monitor started moving. Tony squinted. It was attached to . . .

"A robot?" Tony said, taking a step backward. "Is that a robot?"

"No, Tony Toretto," Rowan said, his voice filled with menace. *"It's your doom."*

CHAPTER 5

Echo slammed on the pedal of her car as she sped toward the beach. The sleek electric hot rod hugged the road tightly, speeding around each corner with a smooth pull, even at a high speed. The g-force of the turns was nothing. She did this stuff every day! Why had it been so hard on the crazy, topsy-turvy pod? And why had it been so much easier for Tony?

Echo's thoughts were derailed as another car—a heavy-looking muscle car polished to an almost mirrorlike state of perfection— roared past her. It was a modern classic style, a wide-framed beast of a car with a custom plate that read T0B1A5. Exactly the kind of distraction Echo needed.

Echo smiled to herself. This was going to be too easy. She angled her foot slightly, and with an electric whine, her car surged up next to the powerful-looking muscle car.

The muscle car eased down, stopping at a red light, and a lanky young man with a mop of curly golden hair leaned over his passenger seat to hit Echo with a lopsided grin.

"Sweet ride!" the smiling youth yelled over the roar of his engine. "Up for a challenge?"

Echo almost laughed. Her car was a hyperfueled custom job engineered by the best mechanics working for Ms. Nowhere. Then she looked at the muscle car again. It had a semitransparent hood, with an array of spinning lights whirling underneath. The wheels had spinners, with another spinner built inside. Everything about the hot rod screamed custom job. Maybe it wouldn't be such an easy race after all. Or maybe that was her lack of confidence, whispering in her ear.

"I guess you're Tobias?" Echo said, based on his license plate.

"You got that right. And I've got more heat on this block than you've got in that toy you're wheeling in."

Echo let the electric engine of her car roar.

"Okay, then, Tobias, let's see what you got!"

The light turned green, and both cars screeched down the road, leaving streaks of black rubber behind them. The two cars sped down the unusually empty beachside highway.

The boy was a skilled driver; that much was obvious. And his car was impressive. But this shouldn't have even been a contest. Echo had proven herself as a driver over and over—and not in some stupid pod test. She had raced *real* cars against *real* racers. Driving was an art form, and Echo was the artist.

A hairpin turn was approaching, and Echo's car hugged the road as always, but she felt her foot easing up on the pedal. Her skin flushed with anxiety. "Weird," she muttered to herself.

She still felt dizzy. The next thing she knew, everything went black. And her car began to spin . . . and spin . . . and spin . . .

CHAPTER 6

Tony narrowly dodged a laser beam from David Rowan's killer robot. It was a clunky silver machine, with two arms and two legs, and a gigantic monitor strapped to its chest. On the monitor was the face of Dr. Rowan.

"You fool!" Rowan cackled cartoonishly. *"You may have cheated your way through the pod, but I have a hundred other inventions to destroy you with! Like these missiles!"*

The robot fired a small barrage of missiles from its shoulders, which tore past Tony and blew a hole in the wall. Rather than wait to see what the robot unleashed next, Tony opted to jump through the hole and get out of the path of destruction. Tony mentally checked where he could be. The hallway that he had been in led to a series of meeting rooms and staff facilities. The hole in the wall should lead directly to a briefing . . .

"Nope," Tony said. "This is totally not right."

It was, in fact, very wrong. The ceiling of the briefing room had apparently been removed and replaced with a series of shifting platforms, each moving in and out of the wall. It was like—

"It's like a video game," Tony whispered.

Another monitor flickered on. David Rowan's angry face appeared. *"That's right! It is a game. A game you can't cheat at. A game you can't win. And when you fail, I'll prove that I am the best engineer to ever grace these halls!"*

"These halls?" Tony yelled. "How did you change the entire building? And where is everyone?"

"I created a distraction, emptying the building so that only we remained," Rowan bragged. *"And I built this entire complex. I designed every wall, every door, every window. And within it, I secretly created the perfect test. The* impossible *test! The test that will lead to your defeat!"*

CHAPTER 7

Echo blinked as she regained consciousness. For a moment, she had forgotten where she was, and had almost expected to wake up and find herself back in that stupid pod.

But instead, Tobias was looming over her. "You okay?" he asked. "You started to spin out."

Echo sat up abruptly, pushing him aside. "My car! Where's my—" It was sitting five feet away, completely intact. Echo's brow furrowed. "How . . . I was spinning out—"

Tobias stood, reaching out a hand to help Echo up. "You pulled out of the spiral just in time. I don't know how you did it, but I've never seen anyone drive like that."

Echo shook off her disorientation. "Seriously? I couldn't have managed that during the test?"

Tobias blinked. "Sorry, what?"

"Nothing," Echo replied, feeling mildly embarrassed. "Thanks, I guess . . . You pulled me out of the car?"

"You looked like you needed some air," he answered. "You okay now?"

"Yeah, I think so. My name's Echo, by the way," she said, reaching out her hand.

"Tobias Grube," he answered as he shook her hand. "You new in town?"

"Not really." Echo looked around. "Where exactly am I? Where is the city?"

Tobias laughed. "You're basically between nowhere and nothing. It's a good stretch to race on, though. Maybe you want a rematch?"

Echo shrugged. "Maybe." But then a slash of lightning in the air distracted her.

In the distance, illuminated for only a second, was an old mansion on a hill.

"What is that place?" she asked.

"Just a dusty old art gallery. Nothing great," Tobias said dismissively.

"An art gallery in the middle of nowhere in

a spooky mansion?" Echo said, with one thin eyebrow raised. "And I'm *not* supposed to go look? I don't think so."

CHAPTER 8

Tony tried to grab one of the old-school emergency phones. Unfortunately, as soon as he grabbed a receiver, David Rowan's robot fired out a pencil-thin laser that severed the physical line.

"Tsk, tsk," Rowan's voice sang through the speakers. *"This game won't be so easily cheated!"*

Tony stepped back, taking in the room. The platforms shifted at a furious speed, but they did so in a rhythm.

"Hesitating, Tony?" Rowan mocked. *"I can see why. A simple race car driver like you could never possibly manage to defeat my doomsday traps!"*

That was the last bit of motivation Tony needed to jump into action, running toward the wall at a breakneck pace. At the last moment before collision, he leaped up and kicked his feet against the opposing wall to his right. He bounced across the narrow hallway, back and forth, letting his momentum propel him upward, high enough to grab the edge of the bottom platform.

That's when Tony heard a whooshing sound and saw a panel in the wall open—and from that panel, boiling water began pouring out, quickly filling the hallway below!

"You can run, Tony Toretto," Rowan said, his voice menacing and low. *"But you can't hide."*

CHAPTER 9

"This is some amazing art," Echo said
as she wandered through the gallery with
Tobias. "Check this one out. It's called *Saira*.
It's beautiful! I can't believe I've never heard
of this gallery. You'd think—" Echo's train of
thought was interrupted by the sound of an
alarm.

And then suddenly the lights went out.

Echo whirled in the direction of a sound.
Something swift swooshed past her with a
rush of air. She couldn't see, but the sound was
unmistakable—a drone!

Echo slapped on the emergency light built
into her spy watch and shined it in a fast
three-hundred-and-sixty-degree sweep.

"Tobias?" she called out, but the stranger
was gone. The drone, however, was as clear
as day: a gleaming black piece of hardware
that would have made Frostee jealous. The

machine had four arms built into it, remote robotics of some kind. More important, it had the *Saira* painting in its polished claws.

"No way," Echo muttered to herself. "A high-tech art robbery?"

She sprang into action, but the drone sailed through the air faster than she could run. Just as she started to sprint, a dozen armed guards surrounded her, stepping between Echo and the escaping drone. A split second later, the remote-control robot rocketed right out a window to freedom, with the painting in tow.

"Hands up!" the guards yelled as they pointed their stun weapons at her. Echo had no choice. In the distance, she could see the robot flying away through the night sky. And then she noticed something weirder . . . The stolen painting was still hanging on the wall!

CHAPTER 10

Tony realized the ceiling was much higher than he'd thought. The moving platforms were the only way up. Down was no longer an option, with the rising level of boiling water filling in.

He glanced down and almost stumbled but steadied himself and jumped once more, grabbing the platform above with an outstretched hand.

"You seriously think that creating a real-life video game is gonna stop me?" the teenager said, laughing. "I rule at games! I play them, like, way too much! Layla even called my skills 'dangerous for my development'! That's how awesome I am."

The voice of David Rowan roared from a nearby speaker built into the wall. *"That's not a good thing!"*

Then circular saw blades spun out of the wall!

"Too slow!" Tony laughed as he dodged them. But one blade came a little too close, and Tony began to slip.

"Getting tired?" Rowan taunted. *"My machines never will!"*

Tony grabbed one of the blades that had lodged in the wall and ripped it free. With a quick spin of his wrist, he flung the serrated metal disk toward a sealed door.

The heavy blade tore through the door and created an exit from the never-ending climb that Tony was struggling with.

Tony dove through the hole, narrowly avoiding another missile attack. He was in a new room now, though it looked pretty much identical to the old one. Tony couldn't help wondering just how big this building was.

And then, with a slight whooshing sound, *another* panel opened and a bunch of snakes fell out. A whole bunch. Like hundreds and hundreds of hissing, writhing, sinister-looking snakes.

"Aaaah!" yelled Tony.

CHAPTER 11

It had taken only a quick call to Ms. Nowhere to clear things up with the security team, though it seemed to Echo as if it had been an eternity. But at least during that eternity, Echo had gotten a sense of who was who and what exactly was going on.

"This is the third painting stolen in the last three weeks!" cried the dark-haired Susan Damon, the curator of the museum. "And every time it's the same! The drone cuts the power, flies in, and flies back out with the art!"

"And they always leave a fake painting in place of the original, too. Plastic replicas!" lamented Ricky Lovas, an elderly man with white hair and a goatee.

"Why leave a fake at all?" Echo replied.

Susan shook her head. "It slows us down usually, trying to find which wing of the museum was robbed. The security grid shows us everything is in place."

"Except this time, there was a witness," Ricky said. "And she saw the drone *and* the criminal. Maybe we can actually catch this guy now!"

"I can trace the drone with my spy watch," Echo suggested. "They're pinging an IP address, and the signal seems to be coming from the south, down the coast."

Ricky frowned. "But the boy—"

Echo shrugged. "If I find the drone, it might lead to Tobias and the paintings. I'll be back soon."

CHAPTER 12

"Interesting," Ms. Nowhere said as she watched the semiconscious, hypnotized forms of Echo and Tony through a monitor. The pair were still whizzing around in circles in the pod, completely unaware that everything they were experiencing was part of a false reality generated by the spinning and the flashing lights.

"The story that each subject is experiencing is created out of their own subconscious," Dr. Rowan explained. "Mr. Toretto doesn't seem to like me very much," he added.

"You were introduced as an authority figure." Nowhere nodded. "His rebellious streak is strong. Echo, on the other hand—"

"Her imagination has created quite an elaborate scenario," Rowan noted as he analyzed the data.

"She's daydreaming about art thieves and mystery stories. Completely on point for her." Nowhere sighed. "Hopefully, both of them can work through their personal demons." She twisted a dial, and the centrifuge spun faster. "I'd hate to see either of them fail," she said.

CHAPTER 13

"You're going to fail!" yelled a twenty-foot-long snake with Rowan's face on it. It wasn't a real snake, of course, but some kind of crazy robot snake that the mad scientist had cooked up. There were also dozens of smaller robot snakes, all trying to bite Tony at every turn.

Tony ran down the long hallway, rounding the corner as fast as he could. Behind him the giant snake slithered along the carpet, propelling its metal form forward.

Without missing a step, Tony pulled his spy watch off, tapping furiously at the buttons on the device.

"You trying to make a call, cheater? Hoping your friends can bail you out? The entire building is cell-signal shielded. You'll have to figure this one out for yourself."

Tony whirled. The robot was almost on him. "Okay, Dr. Snake-bot. Well, how about this, then?" With a quick flip of the wrist, he threw the watch at the snake. It hit the metal forehead of the monster.

Rowan's voice came through speakers built into the robot. *"What exactly did you hope to—"*

Suddenly the spy watch overloaded, sending out a pulse signal. It had been a long shot, but Tony remembered a briefing lesson when they had been taught not to reset the spy watch while they were sitting on a metal surface.

The robot snake emitted a bunch of smoke. All the tiny snakes suddenly died, too.

Tony picked up his watch. It was rebooting, but still functional, luckily. With a quick look, he checked out the hallway he was in. It didn't have the infinitely high ceiling the other did. So . . . where exactly was he supposed to go now?

Then a hatch in the ceiling opened up and a spiral staircase dropped down.

"You built stairs in your super-doomsday tower?" Tony laughed as he launched himself

up the twisting staircase. "You're not even trying anymore!"

Rowan's voice rang out. *"You think it will be so easy?"* he roared.

Suddenly the stairs flattened into smooth slopes. Tony started to slide back down. Now he was in immediate danger of plummeting all the way to the bottom, where a pit of razor-sharp spikes awaited.

CHAPTER 14

Echo traced the drone signal down the coast, all the way to a rickety, waterlogged pier.

She couldn't help shuddering. The location was remote, and the waters off the docks were completely still. The moon was low and gave off little light, but Echo could see a small device duct-taped to one of the rotting timbers.

It was a signal repeater. The signal Echo was following—this was a false trail and probably a trap! Suddenly, Echo's thoughts were interrupted by a very familiar hum.

"Tobias?" she asked as she turned. Though she already suspected what she would see.

Sure enough, three drones swarmed her. They were just like the one she had seen in the art gallery, but instead of hands at the end of their arm attachments, they had—

"Blasters?" Echo said, surprised.

The drones opened fire. It *was* a trap! Echo

jumped to the left, barely avoiding the deadly assault. The wooden structure of the pier swayed under her feet. One of the stabilizing beams must have been shattered by the blasts.

Seeing an opportunity, Echo dove through a freshly created hole in the pier, knowing that the drones would try to follow. Instantly, three of them zoomed through the hole after her. But Echo hadn't allowed herself to hit the water. Instead, she had caught the beam with one hand and twisted her body so that she was nestled safely on a damp beam running horizontally under the pier. It was a gamble. She wasn't really hidden. There wasn't really anywhere to hide. But she wasn't where the drones would expect her to be. All she could do was hope that the machines' momentum would take care of the problem for her.

Mostly, it worked. Two of the drones crashed into the calm ocean, but the third had course corrected. That's when Echo leaped out from the pier understructure and onto the top of the last drone. The hovering machine scanned the water below and, not finding

Echo, concluded that its job was done. Its sensors couldn't register the girl riding on top of it, so it prepared to return itself to its base.

Soon, Echo would find the lair of whoever was stealing the paintings. Tobias, or someone else . . .

CHAPTER 15

Tony tumbled down the spiral staircase toward the spikes. He was dizzy almost immediately. But this wasn't the first time Tony had almost fallen to his doom, and he quickly slapped at his spy watch, unleashing the grappling hook built within.

The grapple fired from the end of the muzzle, and the hook launched up into the distance. The rope went taut. It had latched on to something! Tony pushed a button on the tiny handle, and the thin rope began to retract, pulling him up, out of immediate danger, but toward Dr. Rowan.

Between him and Dr. Rowan, though, was a glass ceiling.

As Tony twisted his wrist in just the right way, his spy watch responded by reeling in the grappling hook and speeding Tony up toward the thin glass ceiling.

Too fast, Tony thought. *Gotta think fast!*

He quickly reached into his pocket and grabbed the first thing he found—a spare spark plug with a hard ceramic and metal housing. Just what he needed! A moment before his body would crash through the glass, he flung the spark plug above him, shattering the ceiling a split second before it would have sliced him to ribbons. Then he sailed through the gap and rolled to his feet.

Rowan was there with a series of computers stretched out in front of him. In his hand was a remote control.

"You . . . you can't," Rowan started to say.

Tony wasted no time and knocked the remote out of the villain's grasp. It plummeted through the hole in the glass floor to the depths of the staircase below.

Tony whirled, ready for the final battle.

CHAPTER 16

Echo rode the drone all the way back to the last place it should have flown to—the art gallery.

More specifically, the warehouse at the back of the gallery. Once she docked into the drone's recharging station, Echo used the light on her spy watch to investigate the dusty, dark building.

There was a lot of odd stuff around—piles of newspapers, a rack of old clothes—but most notably a large printer with a heavy spool of some kind of thin plastic attached to it, and a pile of paintings that looked way too nice to be stored loosely inside a dusty warehouse.

Then Echo heard a familiar voice.

"Tobias?" she called out. Echo looked down and discovered a clear seam in the wooden floor. Pulling on a small hole in the wood, she revealed a hidden staircase.

At the bottom of the makeshift hideaway was the boy she had been seeking. But one look at the teenager, and it was clear Tobias was not the thief.

Echo quickly pulled the gag from Tobias's mouth and untied his wrists. "Are you okay?" she asked.

"I don't know what happened," Tobias said as he rubbed his arms. "Everything went dark and I woke up here, wherever this is."

Before Echo could reply, the drone came back to life. It was clear that it now knew where Echo was, and it was intent on ending her, and Tobias.

"Look out!" Echo yelled, shoving the still-disoriented boy out of the line of fire.

Tapping some buttons on her spy watch, Echo activated a flare that fired across the room. The drone was distracted by the light and spun toward it. Echo didn't hesitate. She jumped at the drone recharging station. It was a long shot, but the charging station was probably the "brain" of the drone. If it wasn't encrypted, her spy watch could override the remote systems!

Echo's watch lit up with the drone controls. Quickly, she sent a command.

The drone floated, then turned to flash a spotlight on a nearby figure—Ricky Lovas!

That's when the art gallery's alarms started blaring, and Echo knew that everything would be over soon.

CHAPTER 17

"You win, okay? Is that what you want? Are you happy now?" Dr. Rowan said, moping.

"Wait. What's happening?" Tony asked, confused. "Are we still fighting?"

"I can't do it!" Rowan said through tears. "I can't beat you! I'm the one who failed."

"Am I supposed to feel bad?" Tony said, even more confused. "You were trying to kill me!"

Rowan shook his head. "It was all just part of *my* test, to see if I could keep working at the agency. I can't even build a security system that can stop a teenager!"

"But the robots and the threats . . ." Tony shook his head.

"Just part of the act. Half of it was holographic projection anyway. None of it could hurt you. When Ms. Nowhere finds out . . ."

"Just hold on. We can work this out," Tony said, patting Rowan on the shoulder in an attempt to comfort the overwrought engineer.

And that's when Rowan grabbed a second remote control—one connected to a long extension cord—and began pressing buttons.

"You foolish child! You thought you defeated me? This robot, my final robot, is truly unstoppable!"

Except that nothing happened.

Rowan looked down at the remote and kept pressing buttons. "I don't understand," he said in a much more subdued voice. "Where's my giant killer robot?"

Tony shrugged, holding up an unplugged extension cord that ran from the remote, which Rowan was holding, to the wall. "I noticed your remote kind of looked like another secret weapon. So when I patted your shoulder, I kicked it from the socket." Tony gave the scientist a lopsided smile. "Sorry, but listen," Tony continued, dropping the cord. "Look at everything you built here! You're an amazing engineer! So I managed not to pass out in the spinning pod. You built it so it could be beaten. Just like you built everything in this building so I could escape it."

"W-well," Rowan stammered. "I mean . . ."

"Like the platforms? Why build those at all if all you wanted to do was win? No, they were there so I could be challenged," Tony said, realizing it now. "You built a great death-trap building! You don't need to defeat me; you're already so winning! Seriously!"

Rowan blushed awkwardly. "Hey, thanks. I kinda did try to destroy you, though."

Tony grabbed the scientist by the shoulders. "Let's let them think you beat me! Only a little, though. So you, like, barely beat me?"

"You would cheat," Rowan asked, his jaw dropping, "to save my job?"

"I guess so. I know you don't like cheating . . . but you *are* a good engineer. You really had me going in there! And together, I bet we could create the coolest video game ever, you know?"

"If you're sure . . . ," Dr. Rowan said, hesitating.

But Rowan's voice was sounding farther away now.

And another, more distant voice of Ms. Nowhere could be heard. "Okay, that should do it. Wake them up!"

And then suddenly everything went white.

CHAPTER 18

"What is the meaning of this!" shouted Susan Damon, the museum's curator, as she burst into the warehouse storage room.

Echo gestured at the pile of paintings. "Check it," she said. "I think you'll find your missing art isn't as missing as you thought. And if you search your employee here, I think you'll find a remote for controlling the drones."

Ricky glanced uncomfortably at the pile. "Those are the fakes," he sneered. "We put them here for now. She'll say anything to save her little friend. She's probably in on it all!"

"Then how about we look at your fingernails," Echo said, pointing. "Those fake plastic paintings? I have a feeling we'll find some of the same plastic used on those 'fakes' under your nails. The same plastic that's hooked up to this printer!"

With that, Echo pulled back the tarp on the printer, unveiling it.

Susan was dumbfounded. "That's . . . you mean . . . ?"

Echo nodded. "The drones never took the actual paintings. Instead, they covered them with a thin plastic fake. Then Ricky would take them out here so he could 'dispose' of them. In other words, sneak them out undetected!"

"But why?" Susan asked, completely baffled.

"What did you expect, Susan?" he yelled. "You know I could run this gallery better than you! Why, I could transform it into a destination gallery of modern art unlike any other! But no, everything always has to be your way!" Ricky pulled a dangerous-looking device from his jacket. A light on the controls began blinking. "Let's see how you handle your way out of this!"

Susan started to argue, but Echo was quick to pull her back. "Wait!" Echo cried out. "That's a cascading pulse bomb! If it goes off—"

"Everything goes boom!" Ricky said, sneering. "All of you, the art, the entire building!"

"Just deactivate the bomb, Ricky," Echo said, trying to sound intimidating. "No one has to get hurt."

"Never!" Ricky said, flinging the bomb and running away. The bomb blinked. It was active. It was going to explode.

Echo almost froze. Her arms and legs felt heavy. Her body wanted to shut down. It was like the pod test all over again, except this time, there was no safety measure to shut it down and no teammate to lend a hand. There was only her, no one else. No one was going to save the day. Unless she did.

Echo leaped into action, grabbing the bomb and running with it. The explosion would be huge, but if she could get far enough away, Tobias and Susan and all the art could be safe.

She could feel the bomb warming up in her hand. She knew it would explode any second.

So she jumped out the window. It was the only way. She would plummet down the cliffside toward the ocean. But everyone else would be safe.

And then everything went white, and Echo was certain this was the end.

Until she heard a voice in the distance.

Ms. Nowhere?

"Okay, that should do it. Wake them up!"

EPILOGUE

The pod slowly ground to a halt. The semiconscious forms of Echo and Tony were carefully removed.

In only a few minutes the pair were awake, and both were completely disoriented.

"It wasn't real?" Tony said moments later. "But it felt . . ." He looked up and saw David Rowan standing nearby. He glanced over at Ms. Nowhere and beckoned her closer. "Are we one hundred percent sure? Because I'm almost positive that guy there might be, like, super evil . . ."

Overhearing, Rowan laughed in a friendly voice as he reached out to shake Tony's hand. "I promise you, I'm not a super villain. I designed the hypnotic pod that induced your dream state. And I have to compliment you, Tony. Your imagination is quite fierce. Maybe we should make a video game together!"

71

"Okay?" Tony said as he shook the offered hand.

"So wait," Echo cut in. "That whole thing where I passed out and Tony did everything himself—"

"A bit of shared consciousness via gentle suggestion," Ms. Nowhere said. "Neither of you was awake inside that pod for more than a few seconds. The rest of the scenarios spun out of your own subconscious."

"Yeah," Echo replied, shaking her head. "I get that. But did we pass the test?"

Ms. Nowhere shrugged. "The test? The spinning machine was just to help induce the hypnosis state. The real test was the choices you made."

Tony jumped in. "But Echo got to race in her test! I didn't get to race! So it's not really fair—"

"It's not a win-or-lose scenario," Ms. Nowhere answered. "You were presented with choices, facing your own strengths and weaknesses. The decisions you made were informative."

"We did beat the bad guys, though," Tony said. "So we must have done pretty good?"

Ms. Nowhere waved her hand dismissively. "Again, it was informative. The data will be examined and added to your profile. If it makes you feel better, neither of you let us down."

"All I know is that I need some sleep," Echo lamented.

"I should have known it wasn't real," Tony grumbled.

And then the conversation was interrupted by a loud crash and a shout.

"Ms. Nowhere! This is outrageous!" Layla yelled, storming in with Frostee and Cisco behind her. She was *mad.* Her hair was also green . . . as was most of the rest of her. And she was covered in feathers.

Ms. Nowhere sighed. "Do I even want to know?"

"In our defense," Frostee began, "we didn't know the paint would fall right where she was standing."

"And the feathers shouldn't have been that sticky," Cisco added.

"I am going to hurt them," Layla fumed. "This is understood, right? One day, when they least expect it."

"All of you get cleaned up or go rest or something. We still have a lot of data to examine and work to do," Ms. Nowhere said.

The group of kids made their way out, though Tony, the last to slip through the door, managed one last question.

"But we won, right?" he asked. "We passed the test?"

Ms. Nowhere pressed a button on her watch, and the door automatically closed in the young racer's face. She dusted off her sleeves and turned to David Rowan.

"This," she said, "is why I didn't become a teacher. Imagine this every day."

"I don't think most teachers place their students in hypnotically induced trances," Dr. Rowan countered.

Ms. Nowhere picked up a data pad and began typing. "The truth of it is they both did quite well. Tony managed to overcome some of his impulsive behavior, plus he showed compassion. Echo overcame her own self-doubt."

"They also both had some red flags," Rowan pointed out.

"They both have great potential, though," Nowhere said. "But it really comes down to which one of them is ready today." She paused over their names on her pad. Then she looked up at Dr. Rowan. "I know who it has to be. There's only one choice, really." She gave a sly smile as she checked a box. "But what do you think?" she asked. "Which one did I pick?"